# National Socialist Racial Policy

## By Nicolas Kinloch

First published 2015 by Searching Finance Ltd,
ISBN 978-1-907720-86-4

Book design and typesetting by j-views, Kamakura, Japan

– iii –

## About the author

NICOLAS KINLOCH TAUGHT history at the Netherhall School and Sixth Form College, Cambridge.

## About Searching Finance

SEARCHING FINANCE PUBLISHES books on economics, finance and politics. For more information, please visit www.searchingfinance.com

# National Socialist Racial Policy
## For Students

## Acknowledgements

THE AUTHOR WOULD LIKE TO THANK Dr Séan Lang, Senior Lecturer in History at Anglia Ruskin University for his editing of the original manuscript, and the late Tom Kowol, Cedric J Harrald and Chris J Mason for their encouragement. He would like to thank Dr Janine Maegraith for her careful reading of the manuscript and for her suggestions for improving it. He is also grateful to Professor David Cesarani and Dr Jo Reilly for their invitation to participate in the symposium *After Eichmann*, held at the University of Southampton in April 2002. Opinions expressed in this textbook are solely those of the author, except where specifically stated otherwise.

# Contents

# Introduction

THIS BOOK IS INTENDED PRIMARILY for A and AS level students, but the author hopes that a more general readership might also find it useful.

No aspect of National Socialist Germany has received more attention in recent years than its racial policy although, as we shall see, this has not always been the case. During its twelve years in power, the National Socialist regime systematically robbed, deported, terrorised and eventually murdered millions of people across Europe. Europe's Jews were from the beginning the pre-eminent victims, but there were others.

Recent years have seen a massive amount of new research into National Socialist racial policy, triggered by the opening of archives in Central and Eastern Europe that were once closed. Many elements have become clearer, but some questions remain stubbornly unanswered. Who, exactly, was responsible for the decision to murder Europe's Jews and when, exactly, was this decision taken? How much did ordinary Germans know about the genocide? Was there, indeed, such a being as an 'ordinary German' in the sense implied by the question? Was the mass-murder of the European Jews, and the accompanying transfer of populations, as mysterious as is sometimes alleged? Or was it part of a rational plan for the economic re-ordering of Europe? How far was the National Socialist elite driven by ideology, and how far by more pragmatic concerns? For that matter, was there ever a coherent National Socialist ideology at all? Was the physical destruction of the Jews always the ultimate aim of the National Socialist regime, or were there always alternative policies that might have been followed? How do National Socialist policies concerning such groups as the 'hereditarily ill' or homosexuals fit into the notion of racial policy?

Some of the questions are not merely difficult: they are and remain intensely controversial. Historians argue fiercely about how far it is permissible to make comparisons between this and other genocides. They cannot agree on whether it is acceptable to examine the catastrophe through the actions of the perpetrators who – inevitably – were almost invariably the initiators of policy and who in consequence produced the bulk of the available source material. Some questions are more than controversial: they can be painful. What exactly was the role of the Jewish councils [*Judenräte*] set up in many of the Jewish ghettos of occupied Europe? Did they simply struggle to ensure the survival of the communities in their care, or did they somehow cross a significant line to become collaborators?

This book does not pretend to provide an answer to all these questions. It is not a history of the Holocaust, and much has had to be omitted. It is a study of the evolution of racial policy, which means that events are mostly seen through the eyes of the perpetrators. There is little here about the struggle for life in the great ghettos of occupied Poland, or the activities of the various resistance groups. Nor will students find much about the German resistance to National Socialism. The response of the Allies to the Holocaust is touched on, but only briefly. Most important of all, there is no space to examine the great Jewish civilisation of Eastern Europe, which had flourished for centuries and was mostly destroyed within a span of eighteen months. Such an examination would have provided a broader context for the second half of the book. It would also have looked at the Jews of Europe on their own terms, rather than simply as 'victims'.

The book does, however, attempt to introduce students to some

*National Socialist Racial Policy*

of the controversies and debates surrounding this important topic. It begins with an examination of how historians have examined racial policy, particularly in recent years. Although the chapter refers to the 'standard view', it should be clear that any consensus is very recent. Historians remain divided on some key aspects of National Socialist racial policy: the chapter reflects this and tries to guide the student through some of the more significant controversies. A second chapter takes a serious look at the ideology of National Socialism and the origins of its racial theories. Chapter 3 looks at National Socialist policy towards the Jews of Germany between 1933 and the outbreak of war. The next chapter takes a wider look at these years, focusing on National Socialist policy towards other groups in Germany: the 'hereditarily ill'; homosexuals; the Romani and Sorb populations and the small number of Germans of African origin whose fate is often overlooked. The next two chapters concentrate on the impact of the war, which with the occupation of Poland in 1939 and the invasion of the Soviet Union in 1941, established racial policy on a continental basis; Chapter 6 analyses the decision-making process and attempts to establish whether, when and by whom a decision for genocide was taken. Finally, Chapter 7 examines the killing-process in detail with a study of the death-camps that were established from 1941. At the back of the book two documents – the Wannsee Protocol and extracts from the telephone log of Heinrich Himmler - are analysed, and there is a glossary. Terms which appear there are highlighted in the text on first appearance for easy reference.

*Introduction*

# Organisation

## The National Socialist Regime (simplified)

Führer and Reich Chancellor: **ADOLF HITLER**, 1933-45; **KARL DÖNITZ**, chancellor, 1945

Vice-Chancellor: **FRANZ VON PAPEN**, 1933

Reich Chancellery: **HANS LAMMERS**

Armed Forces High Command (OKW): **WILHELM KEITEL**

Presidential Chancellery: **OTTO MEISSNER**

> Subordinate offices of the Reich Chancellery included: General Inspector for Highways; Reich Office for Regional Planning; Reich Youth Leadership; General Inspector for the Reich Capital; General Construction Councillor for the Capital of the Movement (Munich)

Reichsführer-SS and Head of the German Police: **HEINRICH HIMMLER**

Head of the Reich Security Main Office: **REINHARD HEYDRICH**

Chief of the Security Police and Security Service: **ERNST KALTENBRUNNER**

Plenipotentiary for the Four-Year Plan: **HERMANN GÖRING**

Privy Cabinet Council (foreign policy): **KONSTANTIN VON NEURATH**

Reich Protector for Bohemia and Moravia: **KONSTANTIN VON NEURATH**, 1939-43 **WILHELM FRICK** 1943 -45

General-Governor of Occupied Poland: **HANS FRANK**

Ministerial Council for the Defense of the Reich: **HERMANN GÖRING**

Reich Foreign Minister: Konstantin von Neurath, 1932-38; **JOACHIM VON RIBBENTROP**, 1938-45.

> Subordinate offices included: NSDAP Foreign Organization (**ERNEST BOHLE**), Reich Office for Foreign Trade

Reich Minister of War: **ADOLF HITLER**, 1938-1945.

Reich Interior Minister: **WILHELM FRICK**. Subordinate offices included: Prussian Interior Minister, Reich Labour Service (**KONSTANTIN HIERL**), Reich Publishing Office, Reich Health Office (**LEONARD CONTI**), Reich Sports Office

Reich Minister for Volk Enlightenment and Propaganda: **JOSEPH GOEBBELS**

> Radio Division: **HANS FRITZSCHE**

Reich Minister for Aviation: **HERMANN GÖRING**

> State Secretary: **ERHARD MILCH**

> NS Flying Corps: **ALFRED KELLER**

Reich Minister of Finance: **LUTZ SCHWERIN VON KROSIGK**

Reich Minister of Justice: **FRANZ GÜRTNER**, 1932-41; **FRANZ SCHLEGELBERGER** (acting), 1941-42, **OTTO THIERACK**, 1942-45

> Civil Law and Procedure Division: **JOSEF ALTSTÖTTER**

> Penal Administration Division: **KARL ENGERT**

Reich Minister for Economics: **WALTHER FUNK** (also Prussian Minister for the Economy and Labour)

Reich Minister for Armaments and War Production: **FRITZ TODT**, 1940-42; **ALBERT SPEER**, 1942-45

> Central Planning Board: **ALBERT SPEER**, **ERHARD MILCH**, **FRITZ SAUCKEL**

Reich Minister for Nutrition and Agriculture: **WALTHER DARRÉ** (also Prussian Agricultural Minister)

Reich Main Office for National Health: **GERHARD WAGNER**

Reich Labour Minister: **FRANZ SELDTE** (also Prussian Labour Minister)

Reich Minister for Science, Education, and Public Instruction: **BERNHARD RUST** (also Prussian parallel ministry).

> Subordinate offices included: Reich Institute for the History of the New Germany, Kaiser-Wilhelm Society for the Encouragement of Science (and the Kaiser-Wilhelm-Institute), Reich Research Council (until June 1942)

Reich Minister for Ecclesiastical Affairs: **HANS KERRL**

Reich Transportation Minister: **JULIUS DORPMÜLLER**, 1937–45 (also Prussian Transportation Minister and Chief of the German Railway).

Reich Minister for the Occupied Eastern Territories: **ALFRED ROSENBERG**, 1941–45

Reich Commissar for the Strengthening of the German Volk: **HEINRICH HIMMLER**

Party Chancellery: **MARTIN BORMANN**

Reich Bank: **WALTHER FUNK**

Reich Commissioner for Health and Sanitation: **KARL BRANDT**

Reich Youth: **ARTUR AXMANN**

Plenipotentiary for Labour Allocation: **FRITZ SAUCKEL**

Reich Ministers without Portfolio: **NEURATH, FRANK, HJALMAR SCHACHT, ARTHUR SEYSS-INQUART**

# The organization of the SS

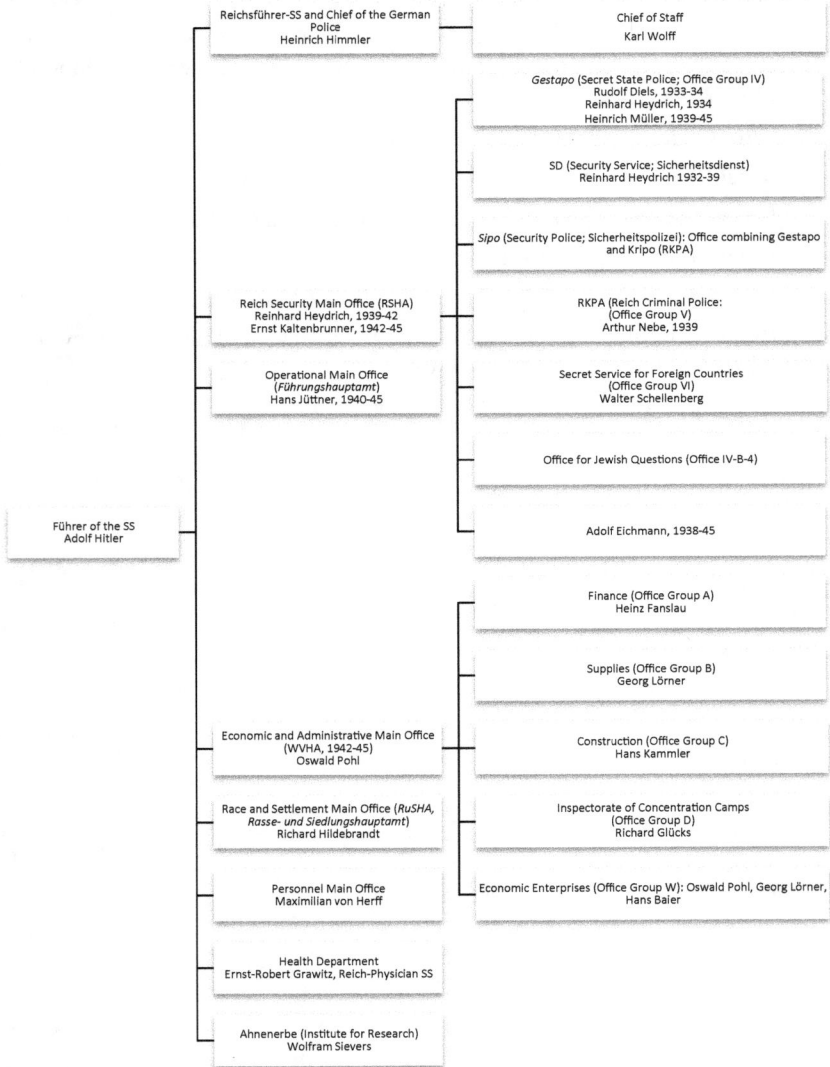

| | | |
|---|---|---|
| | Reichsführer-SS and Chief of the German Police<br>Heinrich Himmler | Chief of Staff<br>Karl Wolff |
| | | *Gestapo* (Secret State Police; Office Group IV)<br>Rudolf Diels, 1933-34<br>Reinhard Heydrich, 1934<br>Heinrich Müller, 1939-45 |
| | | SD (Security Service; Sicherheitsdienst)<br>Reinhard Heydrich 1932-39 |
| | | *Sipo* (Security Police; Sicherheitspolizei): Office combining Gestapo and Kripo (RKPA) |
| | Reich Security Main Office (RSHA)<br>Reinhard Heydrich, 1939-42<br>Ernst Kaltenbrunner, 1942-45 | RKPA (Reich Criminal Police:<br>(Office Group V)<br>Arthur Nebe, 1939 |
| | Operational Main Office<br>(*Führungshauptamt*)<br>Hans Jüttner, 1940-45 | Secret Service for Foreign Countries<br>(Office Group VI)<br>Walter Schellenberg |
| | | Office for Jewish Questions (Office IV-B-4) |
| Führer of the SS<br>Adolf Hitler | | Adolf Eichmann, 1938-45 |
| | | Finance (Office Group A)<br>Heinz Fanslau |
| | | Supplies (Office Group B)<br>Georg Lörner |
| | Economic and Administrative Main Office<br>(WVHA, 1942-45)<br>Oswald Pohl | Construction (Office Group C)<br>Hans Kammler |
| | Race and Settlement Main Office (*RuSHA, Rasse- und Siedlungshauptamt*)<br>Richard Hildebrandt | Inspectorate of Concentration Camps<br>(Office Group D)<br>Richard Glücks |
| | Personnel Main Office<br>Maximilian von Herff | Economic Enterprises (Office Group W): Oswald Pohl, Georg Lörner, Hans Baier |
| | Health Department<br>Ernst-Robert Grawitz, Reich-Physician SS | |
| | Ahnenerbe (Institute for Research)<br>Wolfram Sievers | |

*National Socialist Racial Policy*

# Chapter 1: What is the standard view of National Socialist racial policy, and what errors do students commonly make in examining it?

IT IS HARD to speak of a standard view of this topic, although at the beginning of the twenty-first century there is a growing consensus amongst historians about at least some of its key areas. Most historians, as we shall see, now accept that racial policy – especially towards the Jews – was not predetermined and did not always come from the top. Instead, policy-making was fluid and dynamic, allowing a host of institutions and individuals to contribute to its development. Similarly, a probable majority of historians accept that the role of Adolf Hitler is in no way marginalized or diminished, even if he is no longer seen as the sole decision-maker. There is general agreement that the role of Hitler was central to the unfolding process – to put it crudely, 'no Hitler, no Holocaust'. Hitler repeatedly intervened in policy-making, and always to significant effect. His subordinates 'worked towards' him, doing what they imagined he wanted and looking to his authority to legitimise their decisions. Finally, hardly any historians now imagine, if they ever did, that somewhere in the archives lies a signed document from Hitler ordering the murder of the Jews, Romani or other groups. This was not how policy on such matters was made in the **Third Reich**.

Today we take it for granted that National Socialist racial policy should occupy a large place in the historical consciousness. Many countries, such as Great Britain, formally commemorate the Holocaust on an annual basis, and there are several museums worldwide dedicated to the subject. In many countries it is a compulsory element of the school curriculum. It may therefore be surprising to learn that this concern has not always been the case. Interest in, and knowledge of, National Socialist racial policy was oddly slow to develop, granted the universal shock created by the discovery of the concentration and death camps at the end of the Second Word War. To some extent this was the result of the almost immediate development of the Cold War. Historians and political commentators were generally much more interested in the organisation of the National Socialist state, and specifically about the extent to which it had been totalitarian. In asking this question, of course, they were also examining how far it was legitimate to see comparisons between National Socialist Germany and the Soviet Union, which had replaced it as the enemy. When historians examined the former, it was the elements of modernity that they tended to emphasise. They found it much harder to take seriously the racial theories of National Socialism, which seemed so at variance with their ideas of the Germany of advanced science and technological innovation.

The denazification process in post-war Germany helped confirm to many historians that racial policy was not very important. In completing the various forms and questionnaires that helped them establish their new identity, it was in every German's interest to distance themselves from the policies of the National Socialist regime, and perhaps especially its racial policies. It soon seemed that every German had hidden a Jew or helped one to escape. Denazification forms quickly acquired the nickname of *Persilscheine*, or 'whitewashing certificates'. The desire to minimise adherence to National Socialist racial ideology stretched all the way to the top. Albert Speer, for example, had been Hitler's personal architect and later his Minister of Armaments. In the latter capacity he had employed hundreds of thousands of Eastern slave-workers. One of Hitler's few intimates, he was known as the nearest thing to a friend the *Führer* possessed. Despite this, and despite occupying one of the most powerful positions in Germany, he claimed at the post-war Nuremberg trials that he had never believed in National Socialist racial policies and had known nothing of the mass-murder of the Jews; lies he maintained for nearly forty years. He served a mere twenty years' imprisonment. In a contrast that cannot have been lost on his fellow-Germans, the admittedly unpleasant Julius Streicher – former **Gauleiter** of Franconia and editor of the racist tabloid *Der Stürmer* - was one of the few senior figures who made no attempt to deny his continuing belief in National Socialist racial theory. Despite having held no position of any authority since 1940, Streicher was hanged. Many of the most senior figures, including Hitler, Himmler, Bormann and Heydrich were already dead. This was convenient. Post-war Germans could and did argue that these individuals had been the true believers, and now blamed them accordingly.

Early historians of National Socialist Germany also accepted that racial policy, insofar as it was of any importance, had been the preserve of a few who were not representative of Germany as a whole. Their work often seemed to minimise the extent to which racist ideas permeated every aspect of life under the regime. This reluctance to engage with the significance of racial policy was particularly marked in Great Britain and the United States. A J P Taylor's 1946 polemic, *The Course of German History*, placed Hitler firmly within the German tradition, seeing in Hitler merely the most recent example of a German weakness for powerful rulers. But race was hardly mentioned at all. Alan Bullock's fine biography of Hitler, published in 1952 and subtitled *A Study in Tyranny*, similarly made little reference to racial policy. In 1960 the American journalist William Shirer published his best-selling narrative of the National Socialist period, *The Rise and Fall of the Third Reich*, a book which has never since been out of print. For many readers it was their first introduction to the history of the regime. Again, Shirer's book does not suggest that racial policy was anything other than a peripheral element of the National Socialist movement. In reality, the National Socialist regime represented a decisive break with the past, and its true novelty lay in the importance it attached to race.

It was not until the 1960s that this began to change. The alteration was certainly stimulated by the trial of Adolf Eichmann. Eichmann had been a leading National Socialist official who, during the war, had headed section IV of the **RSHA**. The RSHA was the principal security directorate of the National Socialist regime, co-ordinating the activities of, amongst others, the **Gestapo**, the Security Police and the Criminal Police. Section IV was concerned with Jewish matters, particularly emigration, and in this connection Eichmann had direct responsibility for the wartime expulsion of the Jews from Germany and other countries, and their 'evacuation' to the East, where millions were murdered. After the war, he had succeeded without much difficulty in escaping to Argentina. But in May 1960 he was abducted from Buenos Aires by an Israeli Secret Service unit and flown to Jerusalem. His lengthy trial was deliberately intended by the Israeli government to bring home the horrors of the Holocaust to a new generation of Israelis who had not personally experienced them, and to a world which appeared to have forgotten them. It seems likely that this was much more important to the Israeli government than the fate of Eichmann himself, who in May 1962 was found guilty and subsequently executed.

The Eichmann trial may be seen as the beginning of modern interest in National Socialist racial policy. *Eichmann in Jerusalem: A Report on the Banality of Evil*, a book subsequently published by the American political philosopher, Hannah Arendt, achieved considerable success. Its subtitle meant that 'the banality of evil' quickly became a familiar phrase to describe the perpetration of the Holocaust. Arendt depicted Eichmann as a small cog in the vast bureaucracy of the National Socialist regime. However, recent work on Eichmann - for example, a fine biography by David Cesarani - suggests that Arendt badly misread him. This was no minor official, but an important figure in the **SS** and the **RSHA**, carrying significant responsibility for the planning and execution of policy towards the Jews. By the time he had been in the SS for a few years, Eichmann was suffused with anti-Semitic racism, and saw Jews as an enemy who had to be destroyed. He was no mere cog in the machine, but an ideologist who energetically took the initiative in planning the destruction of Europe's Jews. Arendt had been misled by her belief that National Socialist Germany was a totalitarian state governed by 'rational' and impersonal bureaucrats, as well as by the fact that, in an Israeli courtroom, Eichmann was undeniably lacking in physical distinction or charisma. Despite her flawed interpretation, the world-wide interest in the trial undoubtedly helped to focus attention, almost for the first time, on the racial aspects of Hitler's Germany.

In 1961, at precisely the time that Eichmann was in Jerusalem, Raul Hilberg published his pioneering study of the Jewish genocide, *The Destruction of the European Jews*. This was the first really detailed study of what had happened, and is widely regarded as one of the basic texts of Holocaust studies. Unlike the Eichmann trial, however, Hilberg's work was not well-received in Israel. His focus on the German perpetrators, rather than on the Jewish victims, was not welcomed. And his examination of the role of the **Jewish councils** – set up in most of the ghettos created by the Germans in occupied eastern Europe – caused anger and even outrage. Hilberg appeared to see the councils as little better than collaborators with the National Socialist regime and this was unacceptable to many Israelis. Nor was Hilberg impressed by stories of Jewish heroism in the face of German persecution, observing that, 'The Jews were not oriented towards resistance. They took up resistance only in a few cases, locally, and at the last moment. Measured in German casualties, Jewish armed opposition shrinks into insignificance.' It was not surprising that such conclusions wounded the pride of many Jews, especially perhaps those who were now engaged in the creation and defence of the State of Israel, which fought four wars between 1948 and 1973. Even so, Hilberg's work had a profound effect on studies of National Socialist Germany. For almost the first time, the abundant German records were subjected to detailed scrutiny by a scholar who knew in detail the way in which the National Socialist regime was organized .

Hilberg's work was important because it placed the subject of the Holocaust firmly on the historical map, ensuring that ever since it has been regarded by most historrians as a legitimate topic for enquiry. In addition, from the moment Hilberg's work was published, studies of the Holocaust, and of racial policy more generally, have rested on a secure documentary basis. Hilberg's work also contained some fundamental implications for the future direction of research. It was clear to him, as it has been clear to most historians since, that racial policy was not simply decided by Adolf Hitler, but emerged at least in part from within the bureaucracy of the German party and state organizations. This was an unusual view in 1961. At the same time, Hilberg's view was very different from that of Hannah Arendt. To claim, as he did, that relatively low-level bureaucrats could exercise a decisive influence was far from suggesting that all members of the bureaucracy were much the same, or that ideology or racism did not play a part in their decisions.

Since the 1960s some consensus has indeed emerged amongst historians, though there continue to be many areas of disagreement. The 1970s saw the emergence, outlined below, of two schools of thought about how the decision for mass-murder emerged, and to what extent it was or was not always the intention of the regime to kill at least the Jews of Germany and perhaps of Europe. In part, this debate between **intentionalists** and **functionalists** was a refining of earlier questions that had arisen from studies of the National Socialist regime and how it operated. That debate is not yet over, though probably most modern historians would regard themselves as functionalists to some degree. Whilst the fate of the Jews has remained the principal focus of investigation, since the 1980s there has been a broader examination of the period to include other aspects of racial policy.

Of course, to suggest that a consensus may be emerging is not the same as claiming universal agreement. The work of Götz Aly and Susanne Heim, to take one example, has not found general acceptance. In a book published in 1995, Aly and Heim argued that National Socialist racial policy needed to be fitted into an overall context. In itself, this was uncontroversial. But Aly and Heim contended that the main thrust of racial policy was driven by utilitarian factors, rather than by a racist ideology. In their view, the National Socialist regime was attempting a rational – if morally unjustifiable – reordering of the human resources of the continent to Germany's benefit. This has not been widely accepted, and most historians consider that the authors have underplayed the 'irrational' and ideological, giving too much importance to the academic 'think-tanks' which emerged within such agencies as the **SD** and the **RuSHA**.

The historical consensus was also challenged in 1996, when the American scholar Daniel Jonah Goldhagen published his book, *Hitler's Willing Executioners: Ordinary Germans and the Holocaust*. It became an instant bestseller. The clue to its interpretation of the evidence lay in the sub-title. According to Goldhagen, there were no 'ordinary' Germans. Responsibility for the mass-murder of European Jews could not be confined to elites within the state or Party bureaucracies. Virtually all Germans were afflicted with what he termed 'eliminationist anti-Semitism'. Historians had simply refused to understand that Germans killed Jews because they had always wanted to and because, during the Third Reich, they could. This alone could explain why Germans had continued to kill Jews

*What is the standard view of National Socialist racial policy?*

even at the very end of the war, when it no longer made any kind of sense to do so.

Goldhagen's work was something of a sensation, but in fact it has not aged very well. Historians accepted that he had brought new insights to the phenomenon of the **death marches** of 1945. They also acknowledged that his gruesome accounts of the process of mass shootings restored an element of horror to the Holocaust which was being lost in some of the more clinical examinations of the subject. However, they were quick to point out the numerous flaws in his argument. If Germans had been uniquely infected by eliminationist anti-Semitism, it was difficult to explain why members of other national groups, such as Ukrainians and Latvians, had also participated in the destruction of the Jews. If all Germans had always wanted to kill Jews, it was hard to imagine why they had not done so during the First World War, when many of the areas they were to capture again during the Second were under their control. As some critics observed, the positive experience many eastern European Jews had had of the earlier German occupation contributed, in some cases, to their reluctance to flee until it was too late.

No doubt there will be other challenges to any standard view of this topic. As with all historical subjects, interpretations will continue to emerge as new evidence is uncovered, and long-held views are subjected to new analysis. It is unlikely that the next few years will see a dramatic revolution in the historiography of National Socialist racial policy. Small, incremental changes are much more likely. The consensus is likely to hold, until, rather gradually, it develops into a new one.

# Common student errors

## Assuming that Hitler made all the decisions

IT IS NOT strange that many students believe that all the decisions in National Socialist Germany were made by Adolf Hitler. There seems to be a lot of evidence to support this idea. Students – and teachers, too – often use the word 'Hitler' as convenient shorthand for 'the National Socialist regime'. This is understandable, but it helps to reinforce the notion that Hitler and the regime were one and the same. This, of course, was part of the 'Hitler myth' of the 1930s, a myth designed to enhance Hitler's charisma and authority in the eyes of his supporters. Newspaper reports, film and photographic images all combined to give an impression of a ceaselessly active and omnipotent *Führer* who devoted every moment of his day to securing his mission for the German people. Hitler's subordinates, even important ones such as Heinrich Himmler and Hermann Göring, were often terrified of him and seemed to confirm that it was Hitler alone who counted. 'When there is a decision to be made', said Göring once, 'none of us counts for more than the stones on which he is standing. It is the *Führer* alone who decides.'

The National Socialist leadership principle – the *Führerprinzip* – further reinforced the idea that in Germany, authority flowed from the top, and that Hitler was indeed, as a later title proclaimed him, *Oberste Gerichtsherr* – 'Supreme Law Lord'. In 1939 the Constitutional Law of the Greater German Reich declared:

> The authority of the Führer is total and all-embracing; within it all resources available to the body-politic merge; it covers every facet of the life of the people; it embraces all members of the German community pledged to loyalty and obedience to the Führer. The Führer's authority is subject to no checks or controls; it is circumscribed by no private preserves or jealously-guarded individual rights; it is free and independent, overriding and unfettered.

*What is the standard view of National Socialist racial policy?*

In law, then, Hitler had absolute authority and students might be forgiven for assuming that they were correct to write as if this were so in practice. Besides, some might argue, is there not a moral point, too? If we suggest that Adolf Hitler was *not* the principal source of authority in Germany, might this amount to a whitewash? Does a reduction in Hitler's role and significance not necessarily mean a reduction in his responsibility – even guilt – for the Holocaust and other crimes?

These are reasonable questions, but the fact is that no serious historian in recent years has attempted to exonerate Hitler or to remove from him the principal responsibility for National Socialist policies before and after 1933. To suggest that Hitler was not the sole or even principal decision-maker on every occasion is not to deny that he frequently intervened in policy, and often with decisive results. Although he has been described as a 'weak dictator', this hardly does justice to the reality. As we shall have occasion to see in this book, Hitler persistently radicalised racial policy and encouraged his subordinates to become radical also. As one historian describes it, these subordinates stood between Hitler's claim to charismatic leadership and his need to solve day-to-day problems. In the jungle that passed for National Socialist politics, Hitler's support was an essential requirement in the struggle for authority and power. One way of gaining that approval was always to propose the most extreme solution to any problem, since Hitler almost invariably supported the most radical decision. It was in this way that Hitler set the pattern for the many decisions he did not make by himself.

For despite all the power he undoubtedly held, Hitler was incapable of using it in any systematic manner. In part, this was due to his personal temperament. From his earliest years as a Linz schoolboy, and then as a Vienna dropout, Hitler had always lived an undisciplined lifestyle. He found it almost impossible, at any time in his life, to keep regular hours, or to undertake systematic work. He was uninterested in details and suspicious of expertise.

*National Socialist Racial Policy*

Fritz Wiedemann, one of his adjutants, complained that he often found Hitler prepared to take decisions on very important matters, even without having read the necessary papers. At least this witness found him willing to make a decision. To others, Hitler's unwillingness to decide anything amounted almost to a fetish. Crucial decisions were left unattended whilst Hitler woke only after midday; gorged on cream teas; watched the latest American movie or fantasised about how to rebuild Berlin and transform it into the world-capital Germania. Hitler's belief that many matters simply sorted themselves out if ignored may have had some validity, but it was the despair of his staff and a striking contrast with his arch-enemy Iosef Stalin, with whom he is often compared. Stalin was a paranoid workaholic who attended to every detail of the administration of the ruling communist party and the government of the largest country on the planet. His approach to the exercise of power could hardly have been more different from that of Adolf Hitler. Hitler's personal rule might well be described as government by whim. To give just one example, in June 1938 Hitler happened to see a newspaper report about the trial of two brothers who had held up drivers on one of the new *Autobahnen* and robbed them. Enraged, Hitler demanded that a new law be passed which mandated the death penalty for highway robbery. The law was backdated to cover the period in which the brothers had been active, and the two men were eventually executed. To run a country by reacting to stories in the newspapers might seem bizarre, but this was by no means an isolated example. The story is instructive in another way. It shows that when Hitler *did* intervene, he could do so quickly, decisively and ruthlessly.

If Hitler was simply too idle to make many decisions, how did he manage to govern effectively? One answer is that he governed through two indistinct, overlapping and often competing entities; the Party and State administrations. This is not the place to detail exactly how these functioned, but two points should be understood. One is the importance of Ian Kershaw's view that individuals

**What is the standard view of National Socialist racial policy?**

in both Party and State learned very early to 'work towards the *Führer*'. They did not need, and frequently were not given, detailed policy guidelines to follow. Instead, individuals asked themselves what Hitler would want them to do. Hitler himself asserted that the 'best man' was the one who could sort matters out without coming to him for a decision. The second answer to the question is that it is mistaken to imagine that Hitler's accession in 1933 meant a wholesale change in government. In reality, there was a great deal of continuity. A probable majority of the bureaucracy had never adjusted to the Weimar Republic, and had retained its loyalty to the pre-war German regime which they imagined, mistakenly, that Hitler was about to restore. It was true that a number of bureaucrats, judges, academics chose exile rather than continue to serve. But many of these were Jews, or suspect in others ways, whom the regime had never had any intention of retaining. The rapid destruction of organised opposition also helped ensure that the need for *Gleichschaltung* was never very great. Most government institution quietly co-ordinated themselves and then carried on doing what they had always done. Hitler would find no opposition to his policies from within the German governing elite; and its legendary efficiency would to a large extent make up for the lack of consistent direction that was a permanent feature of National Socialist rule.

## Assuming that National Socialist racial policy was unchanging

IT IS NOT surprising that some students believe that the National Socialists always intended to destroy the Jews, the handicapped and the other victims of their racial and biological obsessions. Until relatively recently, it was a belief widely shared by historians. Such a view is known as **intentionalism**. Historians such as Lucy S Dawidowicz and Gerald Fleming argued strongly that National Socialist racial policy was, from the very beginning, genocidal in intention.

Although a majority of historians no longer accepts this argument, there is some evidence to support it.

Intentionalists pointed *to Mein Kampf*, written in 1924, when Hitler was in no position to translate his threats into reality. In a notorious passage, Hitler asserted that defeat in the First World War would have been avoided if 'ten or fifteen thousand of these Hebrew corrupters of the people had been held under poison gas, as happened to thousands of our best people during the war'. Similarly, in January 1939, Hitler concluded a speech to the Reichstag with the threat that if 'international finance Jewry' provoked another world war, the result 'would not be the bolshevisation of the world and the victory of Jewry but the annihilation [*Vernichtung*] of the Jewish race in Europe.' Hitler himself subsequently referred on several occasions to this speech, significantly re-dating it to the outbreak of war in September 1939. On 19 August 1941, propaganda minister Josef Goebbels wrote in his diary, following a meeting with Hitler:

> We speak about the Jewish problem. The Fuhrer is convinced that his former prophecy in the Reichstag, that if Jewry once again succeeded in provoking a world war it would end with the annihilation of the Jews, is being confirmed. It is being confirmed in these weeks and months with an accuracy that seems almost uncanny.

As Goebbels was writing, German armies were already deep inside the Soviet Union. Alongside them came **Einsatzgruppen**, mobile task forces which, by that time, were routinely executing Jews without regard to age or sex. And in October 1941, Hitler reminded his listeners that he had 'prophesied' that the Jew would disappear from Europe if war were not avoided. By that time, as many as half a million Soviet Jews had already been murdered; by the end of the year that figure had more than doubled. By December 1941 the first Polish death camp was already operational. Intentionalist historians see no reason not to take Hitler at his word. In their view, he threatened the Jews with mass murder and then, when he was in a position to do so, he carried out what he had promised.

**What is the standard view of National Socialist racial policy?**

Not many historians now accept that racial policy was quite as straightforward as the intentionalists suggested. There were certainly problems with their interpretation of racial policy. For one thing, it assumed that Hitler and others always meant exactly and literally what they said. But it is difficult to imagine that when Hitler wrote in 1924 of gassing Jews, he was actually planning the murder of every Jewish man, woman and child on the Continent. Hitler himself warned against regarding *Mein Kampf* as a blueprint. And his January 1939 speech needs to be seen in context. It was made just two months after **Reichskristallnacht**, the nationwide anti-Jewish pogrom which had seen not just extraordinary violence directed against Germany's Jewish community, but a backlash of international protest and condemnation. It seems reasonable to suppose that in his speech, Hitler was effectively warning potential enemies to avoid action against Germany, threatening that any such action would rebound on the very people it was designed to help. The Jews were to be hostages for other countries' good behavior. It seems less reasonable to suppose that it was a prediction of mass murder.

Since the 1970s, most historians have preferred to see racial policy, not as adhering to some notional plan, but instead as dynamic and constantly evolving. Such a view is known as **functionalism**. In this view, no decision for genocide was made until very late in the day. The road to **Auschwitz**, asserted historian Karl A. Schleunes in 1970, was a twisted one. There were many opportunities for even quite low-level functionaries to influence policy, and as we shall see, many did so - a further example of 'working towards the Führer'. The result was incremental decision-making which became progressively more radical. This 'cumulative radicalisation' occurred for a number of reasons. One reason was the very lack of an ultimate goal: it encouraged the exploration of a wide variety of options and policies which often continued even when other decision-makers had abandoned them in favour of something new or different.

Hitler's style of rule also helped this process. Hitler often tasked more than one group with the formulation or execution of policy. In this way he could count on rivalries developing which only he would then be able to resolve. Over racial policy, for example, he could guarantee vicious in-fighting between the SS, the ministries of the occupied territories and the regional party leaders, which did indeed develop. Wasteful though it was in the amount of energy it expended, it had for Hitler the advantage that none of those involved was able or willing to challenge authority since ultimately, they needed his support to defeat the proposals of their rivals. Hitler might be uninterested in details, but he nonetheless insisted on reserving to himself the right to make the final decision in such key areas. And policy tended to become more radical because, as we have seen, decision-makers could generally count on Hitler's support for the more drastic option.

The outbreak of the war also helped to make policy, and especially racial policy, more radical. All the National Socialist leaders agreed that war would allow them to do things that had earlier been 'undreamed of'. War opened up possibilities but simultaneously closed off other, less radical alternatives. For example, one proposal for solving the 'Jewish question' was to re-settle Jews in occupied Poland. But from confining Jews on 'reservations' in Poland to physically destroying them was only a step. Hans Frank, in charge of the **General-Government** [that part of Poland not directly annexed by Germany or the USSR in 1939] showed how thinking was evolving when he reported to a meeting of local governors on discussions he had had in Berlin in December 1941. It is possible that Frank had spoken with Hitler himself. Frank was desperate to clear the General-Government of Jews and had been arguing against the policy of using his fiefdom as a dumping-ground for Jews deported from Germany and the **Warthegau**. After referring to Hitler's 'prophecy' of January 1939, and emphasizing that from now on only the German people should be shown compassion, he asked his audience what they thought would happen to the Jews. Did they believe that they would be lodged in settlements in the East? 'In

*What is the standard view of National Socialist racial policy?*

Berlin we were told, "Why all this trouble? We cannot use them in the **Ostland** or in [Ukraine] either. Liquidate them yourselves !'". It was not possible, he continued, to apply previous conceptions to such a gigantic, unique event. They could not shoot or poison the 3.5 million Jews within their jurisdiction, but some kind of action would be taken that would lead to 'successful destruction'. We do not know the reaction of those who heard him, but it is unlikely that they were surprised. In a significant development the previous month, German Jews had been sent east for the first time, where they were immediately murdered on arrival in Riga. Hundreds of thousands of Soviet Jews had already been shot by this time, a fact that was widely known. The gassing of Jews from the Łódz area had just begun in the first death-camp at Chelmno, even if Frank did not yet know this. The methods of killing would, as Frank went on to indicate, be more fully discussed at an inter-departmental con-ference to be held the following January. Within months of Frank's meeting, the *Aktion Reinhard* death camps of Belzec, Sobibor and Treblinka had been constructed and were operational. The psycho-logical barrier to the carrying out of mass-murder, if indeed there was one, had already been cleared.

Functionalist historians argue that these events did not represent the carrying out of any precise murder-plan drawn up by Adolf Hitler in 1924. Instead, they resulted from many incremental deci-sions over a lengthy period. A range of solutions to what was per-ceived as the 'Jewish problem' was suggested. Some had been ruled out, or were abandoned for other reasons. But others had already been implemented. Each proposal was more radical than its prede-cessor, and each in turn widened the possibilities for what could be proposed in future. All too soon, the 'unthinkable' became a daily routine. Students will find that this book, too, accepts the argument for a functionalist view of National Socialist racial policy.

# Questions

- ❑ Why do historians continue to disagree about National Socialist racial policy?
- ❑ To what extent did Adolf Hitler control racial policy in National Socialist Germany?
- ❑ 'Mein Kampf demonstrates clearly that the mass-murder of the Jews was almost inevitable once Adolf Hiler was in power'. How far do you agree with this assertion?

# Chapter 2: What Did National Socialists Mean By 'Race'?

HOW, EXACTLY, DID National Socialists think about race? What was the origin of their often bizarre ideas? How much did National Socialism depend upon Adolf Hitler's views on the subject, and how far was it influenced by other sources? These are important questions, which lead to others. Do we need to take National Socialism seriously as a political or social philosophy? Did it represent a decisive break with the German past, or was it similar in key respects to what had gone before?

## Race

WHAT IS A RACE? This is a simple question, but a very hard one to answer. It is clear that human beings come in many different sizes, shapes and colours; it is less clear that it is helpful, or accurate, to consider these differences, however marked, as 'racial' ones. All human groups today, however different, are capable of inter-breeding, and producing fertile offspring. So whatever a 'race' might be, it therefore forms part of the human species [*Homo sapiens*], to which all people today belong. Anatomical differences between different groups of people obviously do exist, but these are superficial, and are mostly the result of relatively recent adaptations to local conditions.

Surprisingly, language has often been used to assert the existence of racial characteristics. When Hitler and the National Socialists claimed, for example, that 'Slavs' were sub-human, they obviously meant that those who spoke Slavic languages such as Russian, Czech or Polish were in some elemental way inferior to those who spoke Germanic languages such as German, Dutch or English. However, linguistic differences are even more recent than anatomical ones; both the Slav and the Germanic languages belong to the Indo-European family, suggesting that they share a common ancestry that is at most only a few thousand years old.

Attempts to define humans by 'racial' criteria lead to obvious absurdities. In the United States, for example, people of African descent are usually classified as 'black' regardless of their actual skin colour. People from the Indian sub-continent, however, are generally classed as 'Caucasian' or 'white', irrespective of the fact that many are very dark-skinned indeed. National Socialists in Germany had immense difficulty in assigning a 'value' to people such as the Chinese and Japanese, and never firmly placed them at all in the racial hierarchy. It was not until 1935 that the National Socialist regime even managed to produce a legal definition of what a Jew was. This definition was full of inconsistencies. It turned out that a Jew was anyone who had three or four Jewish grandparents. But it also included people with two Jewish grandparents and who were religiously observant. So what of half or quarter-Jews, the so-called *Mischlinge*? What of the offspring of 'Aryan'-German unions who did not practise Judaism: would they be treated in the same way as those who did? Would it make a difference whether it was the mother or the father who was Jewish? No one really knew: the definition and fate of the *Mischlinge*, as we shall see, was still being discussed at the Wannsee conference in 1942, when over a million Jews had already been murdered and the first death camp had just begun to operate. And what of 'Aryans' who had converted to

Judaism and practised that religion? These would be treated as Jews, but this made nonsense of the assertion that Judaism was solely a racial characteristic.

With these inconsistencies in mind, it may come as a surprise to modern students to realise to what extent virtually all Western societies, not just National Socialist Germany, were organised along 'racial' lines until relatively recently and that this was, more often than not, taken for granted. The United States, to take one obvious example, had permitted both slavery and slave-trading before 1865; after emancipation, it had explicit and legally-sanctioned racial segregation. It was not merely that people of African descent in large areas of the country had no civil rights; they did not enjoy even the most basic forms of legal protection.

It was not just self-interest and their technological superiority that made racists of so many Europeans. Science seemed to confirm their prejudices, and indeed to suggest that they were not prejudices at all. The theory of evolution through natural selection, advanced in 1859 in Darwin's *Origin of Species*, had obvious implications for the study of humankind. Indeed, so clear were these implications that Darwin's next book was to be entitled The *Descent of Man*. Written in 1871, he made clear how he viewed contemporary 'primitive' cultures. Although Darwin opposed slavery and expressed sympathy for 'native' peoples, he evidently did not regard them as equals. On the contrary, one of the expressed purposes of the book was to examine the 'value of the differences between the so-called races of man'. Ernst Haeckel, perhaps Germany's most well-known Darwinist, went still further when he wrote in 1868, 'The difference between the highest and the lowest humans is greater than that between the lowest human and the highest animal.' Haeckel would go on to divide humans into ten different species, with Australian aborigines classified as lowest. It was inevitable that all this would suggest, to some, that 'lower' races would not survive and did not deserve to. In 1896 Rudolf Cronau, a German artist who had travelled extensively in the American West in the 1880s, wrote:

*The current inequality of the races is an indubitable fact. Under equally favourable climatic and land conditions, the higher race always displaces the lower. American Indians naturally succumb in the struggle, its races vanish and civilisation strides across their corpses. Here is again the great doctrine; that the evolution of humanity and of the individual nations progresses, not through moral principles, but rather through the right of the stronger.*

It did not take very long for a still more simplified view of Darwinian principles to take hold of scientific thought. Increasingly life was seen as a primal struggle between the strong and the weak. If 'weak' individuals must perish in the struggle for existence so that stronger and 'fitter' ones might survive, might this not be true of humans too? And the question could be asked still more directly – *should* this not be true of humans too? One German philosopher, Alexander Tille, wrote in 1895, 'Even the most careful selection of the best can accomplish nothing, if it is not linked with a merciless elimination of the worst people'. However, it would take time for such views to become readily acceptable.

## Racial Science In Germany

DURING THE NINETEENTH century racial theory in Germany developed just as it did elsewhere. Following unification in 1871, Germany quickly became the dominant scientific and industrial power in Europe. German universities became famous for their innovative thinking. Developments in such areas as metallurgy, chemistry and the electrical industries meant that German scientists and technologists were soon acknowledged as world leaders. As early as 1868 Darwin wrote that, 'The support I receive from Germany is my chief ground for hoping that our views will ultimately prevail.' However, students should beware of assuming that German scientific progress led inevitably to the National Socialist policies of the 1930s and 1940s. Much thinking had to be done, and some had to be undone, before these policies could actually be put into practice.

*National Socialist Racial Policy*

One key development in racial thinking in Germany was the assumption that heredity effectively accounted for almost every aspect of human society. This was especially true, it was believed, of negative traits such as criminality and asocial behaviour. It was also true of such positive characteristics such as courage, industry and intellectual development. But this had implications for 'unproductive' or 'lower' members of society, as it had for 'lower' races, for if their degenerate state was fixed by heredity, no amount of exposure to higher culture could improve them. If this were so then it led, almost inevitably, to questioning the social and financial cost of caring for those who were genetically or racially inferior.

There was another aspect to the development of Social Darwinist thinking in Germany that had sinister implications for the future. Almost from the beginning, scientists and philosophers alike were agreed that Darwinism had eroded traditional ideas about morality. Theorists such as Georg von Gizycki and Friedrich Jodl argued, in effect, that what was right for the nation or the group was morally right too, a notion the National Socialists would seize. They went further: only what was right for the nation was right in itself. Perhaps the feeling that Darwinism had freed humanity from traditional morality lay behind Hitler's assertion: 'Yes, we are barbarians. We want to be barbarians. It is an honoured title to us. We shall rejuvenate the world. This world is near its end.' On another occasion he declared himself to be the liberator of humanity from 'the dirty and degrading self-mortification of a false vision called conscience and morality.' The Hitler Youth sang that they needed 'no Christian virtue' and wanted to be 'pagans once again'. Agnostic though he was, very little of all this had been intended by Charles Darwin. But it happened anyway.

## The National Socialist World-View

IT SHOULD NOT BE IMAGINED from the above that Hitler, Himmler, and other National Socialists had necessarily paid much attention to developments in racial science. True, enough of the views of Haeckel and other Darwinists had filtered down to affect, often quite profoundly, the mental outlook of many Germans. But it is much more likely that the specific views on race and heredity of the National Socialists came from rather less intellectually-demanding sources. We cannot be certain where Hitler got his ideas from, though much of what he believed about the 'Aryan' and Germanic peoples was commonplace amongst ultra-nationalist groups at the turn of the century. His views on the Jews were equally widely shared and, despite his claims, unoriginal. We do not know exactly what he read during his period in Vienna between 1908 and 1913. His reading – which everyone agrees was voracious, if unsystematic – is likely to have included what in *Mein Kampf* Hitler describes as 'anti-Semitic pamphlets', bought 'for a few pence'. Such pamphlets might well have included material by one of the more popular peddlers of 'Aryan' supremacy, Adolf Lanz. Lanz, styling himself Baron Jörg Lanz von Liebenfels, was amongst the many who claimed to have 'given Adolf Hitler his ideas'. Since he also boasted that Lenin had been one of his disciples, there is legitimate suspicion of this claim. Lanz edited and largely wrote a magazine, *Ostara*, which publicised his bizarre notion of human life as an epic struggle between the blond and dark races, and carried such arresting headlines as 'Are You Blond?' As well as *Ostara*, he also published a book in 1905, *Theo-zoology or the Lore of the Sodom-Apelings and the Electron of the Gods*. Even the title suggests that he may not have been wholly sane. The book was an extraordinary jumble of material about the mythical origins of humanity and especially of Nordic humanity. Lanz claimed that, over the millennia, the 'Aryans' had been weakened by continuous inter-breeding with more primitive forms of humanity. In addition, the Industrial Revolution had been damaging, as 'Aryans' needed close contact with nature: what the National Socialists were later to call *Blut und Boden* – blood and soil. Lanz asserted that the time for an 'Aryan' revival was now at hand. But the inferior races, and the lower social classes whose blood had been corrupted,

*National Socialist Racial Policy*

must be eliminated if this revival were to take place. Judaeo-Christian concepts such as pity for the weak would have to disappear. So would ideas such as socialism, democracy and feminism. Women, in particular, were more passionate than men and more likely to be seduced by those of inferior race. They would have to be controlled by strong, 'Aryan' husbands. Castration and sterilization would also have to be used to rid the world of the threat posed by the socially and racially sub-human

We cannot be sure how much of all this Hitler read, if any. Heinrich Himmler, however, was another matter. Much of what Himmler attempted to achieve suggests an all-too-literal reading of Lanz's fantasies. In 1937 for example, speaking of how he recruited members of the SS, Himmler stated:

> *Only good blood, Nordic blood, can be considered. I said to myself that should I succeed in selecting as many men as possible from the German people, a majority of whom carry this valued blood, it would be possible to create such an elite organization which would successfully hold its own in all cases of emergency.*

Lanz founded the mysterious Order of the New Templars in1908, the same year he claimed to have met the youthful Hitler. The New Templars was an organisation sworn to promoting the centrality of race in human affairs, and its symbol was the hooked cross or swastika, a device later adopted by many similar groups as a symbol of racial purity, though Lanz himself seems to have seen it as a symbol of the divine 'fire-whisk' which, according to Nordic mythology, had cleared the earth at the end of the last ice-age. By 1918 the swastika was the preferred symbol of several of the ultra-nationalist *Freikorps,* who were used by the new republican government to put down the communist rebellions which followed the end of the First World War. If Lanz had any other influence on the infant National Socialist movement though, it was indirect. Lanz was never won over to the Hitler cult, believing Hitler to be himself a racial mongrel. In turn Hitler never credited Lanz with having influenced him, and indeed, had not much interest in the occult elements behind Lanz's bizarre mythology; he left that sort of thing to Heinrich Himmler. Indeed, Lanz was forbidden to publish following the *Anschluss* with Austria in 1938; Hitler may by then have been unwilling to share the credit for his racial 'discoveries' with anyone else. He may even have been embarrassed by Lanz's more absurd flights of fancy.

One person who undoubtedly did have an influence on Hitler was Houston Stewart Chamberlain. Chamberlain had become celebrated in Germany after the 1899 publication of his book *The Foundations of the Nineteenth Century*. An Englishman, he became a German citizen during the First World War and married into the family of the nationalist composer Richard Wagner. Although Chamberlain rejected Darwinism, he fully accepted the notion that some races were superior to others. It was clear from his writings that he believed that it was the Germanic people who had contributed most to the development of European civilisation. Unlike Lanz, Chamberlain was a great admirer of Hitler, whom he knew personally through his Wagner connections. He was an early member of the NSDAP and one of the few who was intellectually and socially distinguished. When he died in 1927, Hitler attended his funeral, a clear mark of Chamberlain's influence on the fledgling National Socialist movement.

Hitler was much less influenced by Chamberlain's self-proclaimed successor, Alfred Rosenberg, who in 1930 attempted to bring Chamberlain's work up to date with his *Myth of the Twentieth Century*. Like so many of the National Socialist elite, Rosenberg had not even been born in Germany: he was from Tallinn, Estonia, then part of the Russian empire. He joined the NSDAP in 1919 and by 1921 was editor of the Party newspaper, the *Völkischer Beobachter*. He found time, in 1929, to found the League for the Struggle for German Culture. He would eventually be the ineffectual Minister for the Occupied Eastern Territories and would end on the gallows in Nuremberg, in October 1946, as a condemned war criminal. His book was admired in some National Socialist circles - Goebbels declared that, 'Say what you like, the man can write' – but Hitler himself was reported to have found it a 'plagiarised piece of junk, bad Houston Stewart Chamberlain'. Rosenberg's main aim had been to promote the idea that the *völkisch* state was the highest good and that its German form was supreme, based as it was on the notion of 'blood-cleanliness'. He affected to despise the French in particular for bestowing citizenship on inferior racial elements, simply because they happened to have been born in the country. Although Rosenberg saw himself as the leading racial theoretician of the National Socialist movement, he was unable to transform this into a lasting position of authority. Even so, he came as near as anyone to formulating a clear response to the question of what National Socialism understood by race.

## The Racial Hierarchy

IN THE NATIONAL SOCIALIST WORLD-VIEW, and indeed that of many Germans who were not necessarily supporters of the regime, there was a clear hierarchy of races. Jews were not contained within this hierarchy: as an anti-race, they existed outside it. The highest element in it was the Nordic. Many racial scientists identified these with the 'Aryans', a rather ill-defined concept. 'Aryans' famously had blond hair and blue eyes, but there was more to them than this. According to Hans Günther, a racial scientist writing in the 1920s, judgment, truthfulness and energy were the qualities which distinguished the Nordic man. He continued, 'The sense for reality, the energy, self-reliance and boldness of the Nordic race are one reason why all the more important statesmen in European history would seem, judging from the portraits, to be Nordic.' What distinguished them from all other races was their unique capacity to create civilisation. No one was quite sure where these 'Aryans' came from, though most agreed that they had moved out of central Asia at some time in the remote past. Himmler favoured Tibet as their original homeland, and in the 1930s sent at least one *Ahnenerbe* expedition there to establish what kinship there might be between Tibetans and modern Germans. According to Hitler, the 'Aryan' was:

> The Prometheus of mankind, from whose shining brow the divine spark of genius has at all times flashed forth, always kindling the fire which, in the form of knowledge, illuminated the dark night. As a conqueror, he subdued inferior races and turned their physical strength into organised channels under his leadership, forcing them to follow his will and purpose. While he ruthlessly maintained his position as their master, he also maintained and advanced civilisation. Should he be forced to disappear, a profound darkness will cover the earth; within a few thousand years human culture will vanish and the world will become a desert.

Of course, not all Germans were 'Aryans'. There had been too much racial mixing. It did not escape popular notice that few of the leading National Socialists, including Hitler, bore much resemblance to the 'Aryan' ideal. One National Socialist *Gauleiter*, Forster of Danzig-West Prussia commented on the *Reichsführer-SS*, 'If I looked like Himmler, I should not speak of race at all.' But Himmler himself believed that a long-term programme of selective breeding, based on his SS, would correct the racial imbalance in Germany. Below the 'Aryan' came the ordinary German. It was not quite clear exactly who these were; there was the same level of confusion as there was about most aspects of racial thinking in Germany. Clearly the term 'German' included all those who spoke German as a first language, meaning not just those in Germany, Switzerland and Austria, but also substantial minorities in Italy, Poland, Czechoslovakia, the USSR and Romania. The term could also be stretched to include those who spoke Germanic languages such as Danish, Swedish, Norwegian, Dutch, Flemish and English. However, linguistic criteria alone were insufficient. The largest English-speaking nation was the United States, but Hitler and his subordinates did not regard it as a Germanic country; it had become too 'mongrelised' and, in Hitler's eyes, too dominated by a Jewish **plutocracy**. That such views mattered was demonstrated in December 1941, when Hitler declared war on the United States without apparently considering its enormous economic and military potential; the 'hybrid' Americans did not deserve his respect.

Below the Germans came the other European groups, notably the 'Latins' or Mediterraneans. Hitler despised the French and considered the Italians to have degenerated since the great days of the Roman Empire. He admired Mussolini, but suspected that the Italian people would not prove worthy of him. The events of July 1943, when Mussolini was overthrown, in Hitler's eyes fully justified this pessimism. However, the Latin peoples, however degenerate, were far above the Slavs in the National Socialist hierarchy. Slavs, put simply, are those peoples who speak the Slavic languages. These include Russian, Polish, Czech, Slovak, Serbo-Croat, Ukrainian and a host of others. It is, therefore, a purely linguistic category. There is no evidence whatever that Slavs form any kind of separate 'race'. Slavs are as likely – or as unlikely – to be blond or blue-eyed as any of the Germanic peoples. Indeed, Slavs and Germans have lived amongst each other for centuries, and have accordingly intermingled. In the Waldviertel, for example, the area of Austria from which the Hitler family came, there had always been a significant Czech presence, and – granted the difficulty of tracing Hitler's ancestry – there was no guarantee that the *Führer* himself was entirely free from the 'taint' of Slavic blood.

There were several reasons why National Socialists placed Slavs in the 'sub-human' category. One was the traditional rivalry that had existed since the nineteenth century between Slavs and German-speakers within both Germany and the Austria-Hungary. In Germany there was a notable Polish presence, especially in Silesia and West Prussia. By the turn of the century in Austria-Hungary, antagonism between Germans and Czechs in particular had reached chronic proportions. It is highly likely that Hitler had absorbed this dislike of the Slav element within his native Austria. His antagonism to the Habsburg rulers of Austria before 1918 grew from his conviction that they were 'selling out' to the Slavs, and his dislike of Austria stemmed in large part from his belief that the German element there was being submerged by successive waves of Slavic immigration.

Traditional fear and dislike of Russia, the biggest Slav nation of all, also lay behind this contempt. Such hostility was dramatically increased when, in 1917, Russia became communist following the Bolshevik revolution. Before 1917, it was common in Germany – and elsewhere - to regard Russia as a backward nation of robotic peasants, but one at least controlled by a ruling class that was partly Germanised. Several early members of the NSDAP, such as Alfred Rosenberg and Max von Scheubner-Richter – the latter was killed during the 1923 Beer Hall Putsch - were themselves members of this German elite in Russia. Now its influence had been swept away and replaced, in the eyes of Hitler and many of his contemporaries, by a sinister and Jewish-dominated regime. Such a regime, in their view, would bring out the worst characteristics of the sub-human mass of the population. Events in Russia after the revolution offered, in Hitler's eyes, graphic proof not only of the dreadful effects of 'Jewish-Bolshevik' rule, but incontrovertible proof of the inferiority of the Slav. A leaflet, *The Sub-human*, produced by the RuSHA in 1942, warned Germans of the true nature of their enemy in the East:

> *The sub-human, that biologically seemingly complete similar creation of nature with hands, feet and a kind of brain, with eyes and a mouth, is nevertheless a completely different, dreadful creature. He is only a rough copy of a human being, with human-like facial traits but nonetheless morally and mentally lower than any animal. Within this creature there is a fearful chaos of wild, uninhibited passions, nameless destructiveness, the most primitive desires, the most naked vulgarity. Sub-human, otherwise nothing. For not all that bears a human face is equal. Woe to him who forgets it.*

Still another reason for the relegation of the Slav peoples to a low status in the racial hierarchy was that their land was coveted. Hitler had dreamed for years of establishing **Lebensraum** in Russia, stating in *Mein Kampf* that 'when we think of the East, we think primarily of Russia and her vassal border states.' As sub-humans, Poles and Russians lost any title to their land, just as Native Americans and Aboriginal Australians had done in the previous century. Those planning the future of German-occupied Russia estimated that perhaps 30 million Russians would have to emigrate or starve if the land was to be settled by Germans. The rest would be slaves, working for their German masters. They would be given sufficient education to read German traffic signs and thus avoid getting themselves run over. In 1941 it seemed that this empire in the East was on the verge of being realised. It was Göring who announced the sort of rule he had in mind for the Slav: it meant shooting those who looked sideways at their German masters. It was a paradox that when the Germans did move east, they often encountered considerable initial support from the local populations, especially in the Baltic states and Ukraine. They were often seen as liberators from communist rule. Ukrainians, in particular, hoped that Hitler would support some sort of separate Ukrainian state, even if it were one under German 'protection'. It is possible to argue that, if Hitler had supported such moves, he could have won the war in the East. But in July 1941 he made it clear, at a meeting at Angerburg with Rosenberg, Göring and others, that he had no intention of allowing any form of self-government by the peoples of the East. On the contrary, he informed his listeners, they could now proceed with the shooting and resettling that would be necessary for the 'final solution' there.

What was below the Slav? The answer was virtually everyone else, and certainly the brown and black races. There was nothing especially National Socialist about this: as we have seen, many Europeans and Americans thought in much the same way. There was some dispute about exactly where the Chinese and Japanese stood in the hierarchy: on the whole the NSDAP's racial experts were inclined to classify them as sub-humans. There was a long tradition of German antipathy towards what was known as the 'Yellow Peril', most famously expressed in 1900 when Wilhelm II, sending troops to help suppress the Boxer rebellion in China, had urged them to take no prisoners and act in such a way as to ensure that no Chinese should look 'cross-eyed' at a German in the next thousand years. However, this was a difficult position to support in the case of the Japanese, who had emerged as a Great Power following their defeat of Russia between 1904 and 1906. More important was the fact that it was politically inexpedient: in November 1936 Germany signed the Anti-Comintern Pact with Japan, a treaty ostensibly directed against international communism but in practice against the Soviet Union. Whatever doubts racial theorists might have had about the Japanese, it was clearly unwise to be too specific as long as Japan's friendship was necessary. For the time being, therefore, the Japanese, at least, were counted as 'honorary 'Aryans'; one more example of the impossibility of establishing any kind of rational policy based on race.

## The Jews

STRICTLY SPEAKING, THE JEWS were not a part of the racial hierarchy, but stood outside it. Of course, anti-Semitism in Germany did not begin with Adolf Hitler, nor was it unique to Germany. The nineteenth century saw a gradual increase in anti-Jewish sentiment in Europe, at the same time as – and in large part because - legal and state discrimination was weakening. However, students would be mistaken if they imagined that there was anything especially alarming in this for German Jews. On the contrary, most observers at the time thought that Germany was one of the safest places in Europe for Jews. During the First World War, one German Jewish philosopher, Hermann Cohen, claimed, 'Despite the universal contrary prejudice, I venture to assert that in Germany equal rights for Jews have deeper roots than anywhere else.' German unification in 1871 had brought full citizenship to German Jews, leading a Jewish member of the Prussian Reichstag to assert that 'finally, after years of waiting, we have arrived in a safe harbour.' German Jews made a large contribution to developments in the arts and sciences, as well as to the German empire's expanding industrial and technological base. So promising seemed the situation of Germany's Jews that the country became a magnet for Jews from other countries. This was particularly true of those fleeing sometimes state-sanctioned persecution in Russia from the beginning of the 1880s. There, **pogroms** were commonplace. Hundreds might be killed during these outbreaks, as happened later in Kishinev in 1903. Pogroms were not spontaneous outbreaks of popular feeling; they were carefully initiated, organised and controlled by state authorities, something the National Socialist regime remembered and re-instituted when they captured many of these same areas in 1941. In many parts of the Baltic states and Ukraine the German occupiers could and did confidently leave anti-Jewish actions to the local population. In this way Latvians, Lithuanians and Ukrainians, too, found themselves 'working towards the *Führer*'.

If Russia was dangerous for Jews, so too was France. This may be surprising, as the Revolution had seemed to clear the last vestiges of anti-Jewish legislation from the country. But the Abbé Barruel, writing only a few years afterwards, alleged that the revolution itself had been a conspiracy led by Freemasons and Jews. Such claims were widely believed. Despite many changes of regime during the nineteenth century, anti-Semitic feeling remained very strong in France, as the **Dreyfus Affair** would demonstrate in the 1890s.

The anti-Semitism of the later-nineteenth century was different in important ways from that of earlier periods. There had been ferocious attacks on Jews in medieval Germany, notably when the Crusading armies passed through on their way to the Holy Land in 1098. Jews in many, perhaps most, countries in Europe experienced periodic persecution when they became the target of government or community-inspired violence. Several countries, such as England in 1290 or Spain in 1492, had expelled their Jewish populations altogether. During the Black Death, the great plague of the fourteenth century, Jews were accused of poisoning wells. In February 1349, two thousand Jews were murdered in Strasbourg. In August, the Jewish communities of Mainz and Cologne were destroyed. By 1351, over two hundred Jewish communities in Europe had been wiped out. Such actions were usually attributed to religious motives, but there was also a strong element of economic calculation too, especially where rulers had borrowed money from Jews. Religious anti-Semitism continued well into the modern period. Martin Luther, the principle agent of the Protestant Reformation, was a violent anti-Semite. Many Catholics agreed with him in this, if nothing else, and anti-Semitism continued even beyond the Enlightenment of the eighteenth century. It survived the creation of a united Germany in 1871, when for the most part legal restrictions against Jews were lifted. The long pontificate of Pius IX [1846 – 78] saw an increase in anti-Semitic statements from the Vatican. The Jews, claimed the Pope, had no God but their money, whilst on another occasion he described Jews as dogs, of whom there were 'too many of them at present in Rome, and we hear them howling in the streets, and they are disturbing us in all places.' Such propaganda clearly gave support to Catholic anti- Semites in Germany. Between 1867 and 1914 there were fourteen prosecutions of Jews accused of the 'blood libel', the widespread delusion that Jews carried out the ritual murder of Christian children. Nonetheless, it was a clear sign of the waning importance of religious anti-Semitism that none of these prosecutions was successful, and that several leading German churchmen protested about them. And religious anti-Semitism, however terrible its effects had often been, did not suggest that Jews were permanently and unchangeably different. Jews who converted to Christianity ceased, by definition, to be Jews.

But by the late nineteenth century, 'the Jew' was seen increasingly as a _biological_ rather than as a religious phenomenon. In this view, the Jews were a race, or at least a nation, and Judaism was transmitted through the blood. It followed that Jews did not cease to become Jews simply by ceasing to practise the rituals of the Jewish faith or by converting to Christianity. Indeed, the 'assimilated Jew' was seen as in many respects the most dangerous kind of all; there was a real risk that such Jews might be mistaken for non-Jews, and thus make more likely the worst crime of all – racial 'mixing.' Hitler wrote in *Mein Kampf* that 'the dark-haired Jewish youth lies in wait for hours on end, satanically glaring at and spying on the guileless girl he plans to seduce, adulterating her blood and removing her from the bosom of her own people'. Seduction could be indirect. It was the Jew, claimed Hitler, who had brought Negro soldiers into the Rhineland with the idea of 'bastardising' the white race and lowering it to a level where the Jew could dominate it. Despite the progress Jews had made in late nineteenth-century Germany, they still faced much discrimination. The economic crash of 1873 was widely blamed on Jewish finance, despite the fact that Jewish bankers and financiers suffered as badly as any one else. The most important Jewish banker in Germany, Gerson Bleichröder, had in fact repeatedly warned of the likelihood of the 1873 disaster, but this did not prevent widespread accusations that he had somehow both organised and benefited from it. Thereafter, anti-Semitic propaganda, groups and political parties proliferated. The same was true in Austria-Hungary. Pan-Germans such as Georg Schönerer argued in 1885, 'In order to carry out the reforms we seek, it is imperative that Jewish influence in all areas of public life be eliminated.'

Karl Lueger was mayor of Vienna from 1897 until his death in 1910. Lueger, leader of the Christian Social Party, was a direct inspiration to the young Adolf Hitler, who admired his powers of oratory as much as his anti-Semitism. Lueger, according to a contemporary, 'knew how to make himself appear personally the embodiment of anti-Semitism in the mind of the public'. Lueger believed that 'the Jews are not the martyrs of the German people, but the Germans are the martyrs of the Jews'. Next to these beasts in human form, he claimed, 'wolves, lions, panthers, leopards and tigers are human beings'. Hitler greatly admired Lueger, writing in *Mein Kampf* that Lueger had appreciated that in anti-Semitism lay the salvation of the state. However, he criticized the fact that Lueger's anti-Semitism was essentially based on religion, and not race: 'If the worst came to the worst, a splash of baptismal water could always save the business, and the Jew at the same time'. He also thought that Lueger's outlook was too narrow: Lueger saw the Jews as a threat to Austria but not, as Hitler believed was the case, to humanity as a whole.

Historians disagree about exactly when Hitler became an anti-Semite. Despite his later claims, there is some evidence that he had reasonably good relations with the Jews he encountered in Vienna during his 'dropout' period before 1913. The suggestion that he feared that he himself was of Jewish origin – a rumour widely put about by his political enemies – does not seem to be based on much evidence. It is true that he did not know who his paternal grandfather was, but he was unlikely to have been Jewish. Hans Frank claimed after the war that he had seen evidence for this and had even turned it over to Hitler, but this was almost certainly un-true. Whatever the truth, Hitler certainly was a violent anti-Sem-ite by the end of his service in the First World War. The 25 Point Programme adopted by the NSDAP in 1921 excluded Jews from the *Volk* community and stipulated that no Jew could be a German citizen. *Mein Kampf* also contains many grossly anti-Semitic refer-ences. Jews were blamed simultaneously for upholding the capitalist system, and for attacking it through such inventions as Marxism. Hitler expressly blamed the Jews of Germany for undermining the home front in 1918, and for establishing the Weimar regime he hated. Hitler, of course, was far from unique in believing this. The former German emperor Wilhelm II wrote to Field-Marshal von Mackensen in December 1919 that his abdication the previous year had been 'the deepest, most disgusting shame ever perpetrated by a person in history'. The Germans had inflicted this injury on them-selves, but they had been 'egged on and misled by the tribe of Juda'.

**National Socialist Racial Policy**

No German should ever forget it, nor rest until these 'parasites' had been eradicated from German soil. The ex-emperor went on to state his belief that there should be a world-wide 'Russian-style' pogrom against the Jews, who were a nuisance who would have to be got rid of eventually. His own view was that gas would be the most effective means.

'The Jews', Hitler once said, 'are undoubtedly a race, but they are not human.' Jews were in fact perceived as an anti-race: a grotesque and lethal perversion of humanity. This helps to explain the extraordinary virulence of National Socialist anti-Semitism. Jews were racially and hereditarily disposed to be anti-German and, indeed, opposed to the very idea of civilisation. The Jew, Hitler declared, was incapable of creating civilisation, but could only live on it in a parasitic, and ultimately destructive, fashion. In National Socialist propaganda, Jews were regularly compared with plague bacilli and other dangerous microbes. A recent writer, Stephen J Glass, considers that National Socialist hostility to Jews amounted to a phobia. 'We can live without them', Hitler remarked during the war, 'they can't live without us'. Hitler demonstrated his pathological view of the Jews throughout *Mein Kampf*, claiming that wherever the Jew established himself, the host people was bound to be bled to death eventually. The Jew, in Hitler's eyes, 'poisons the blood of others but preserves his own unadulterated'. He returned to this theme in the very last words he ever committed to paper, when in the 1945 Political Testament he referred to 'international Jewry' as the 'international poisoner of the peoples', and urged his successors to ensure rigorous adherence to Germany's racial laws. By then, nearly six million Jews had been murdered: 'sub-human' Soviet troops were only a few hundred metres from his bunker. The Testament, and the circumstances under which it was written, was a telling comment on the power of Hitler's anti-Semitic and racial obsessions.

# Questions

- To what extent was Charles Darwin responsible for the development of National Socialist racial theory?
- Why did so many Europeans in this period believe that a racial hierarchy existed?
- Why were National Socialists anti-Semitic?

# Chapter 3: How Did Policy Evolve Towards The Jews 1933 – 39?

THIS CHAPTER LOOKS at how National Socialist policy towards the Jews of Germany evolved after 1933. Who was in charge of this policy, and why did it develop in the way it did?

Well before what National Socialists called the 'seizure of power' in 1933, many Germans believed that the presence of half a million Jews in Germany constituted a problem which would have to be solved. The racial theorist Hans Günther, writing in 1927, concluded his book *The Racial Elements of European History* by asking whether Germans had the courage to make ready for future generations a world cleansed racially and eugenically, and suggested that the solution lay in the separation of the Jews from the rest of the population.

Once Hitler was in power, an ever-increasing number of organisations and individuals would find themselves in competition with one another over Jewish policy. Not all of them were always driven principally by ideology, although it would be unwise to underestimate the level of anti-Semitism that existed. For some, staking a claim to the formulation of Jewish policy was one way of ensuring that they had some say in an area that would obviously be of growing importance. There were advantages for Hitler in this chaotic situation. His power was greatly enhanced: only he had the authority to decide amongst the competing claims for control of racial policy. In the short term, however, it meant that there was almost no such thing as a co-ordinated policy against Germany's Jews.

Adolf Hitler was appointed chancellor in January 1933. Almost immediately Jews began to leave Germany. Orchestral conductors Otto Klemperer and Bruno Walter went abroad because, as the Frankfurter Zeitung newspaper put it, it was impossible to protect them against the mood of a German public who had been provoked by 'Jewish artistic bankrupters'. They were followed by a dazzling array of talent, including Albert Einstein, who on an official list was named an enemy of the state, described as 'not yet hanged'. Other noted scientists forced into exile were Erwin Schrödinger, Viktor Hess and Gustav Hertz, all Nobel Prize-winners, as well as Hans Bethe and Max Born. Also forced abroad was Emmy Noether, whom Einstein regarded as the greatest female mathematician who had ever lived, as were the novelist Thomas Mann [who was 'Aryan', but married to a Jewish wife] and the film directors Fritz Lang and Billy Wilder.

What may seem strange is that more Jews did not leave, but the explanation is clear. First, few foreign countries were willing to receive any but the most eminent refugees – Albert Einstein, for example, ended up in Princeton. The Depression was still the dominant fact of international life. At a time of high unemployment, governments feared a backlash if they were seen to be giving a welcome to large numbers of foreign Jews. Second, it was not yet clear that there would be no place for Jews in Hitler's Germany. Jews had experienced persecution many times before. Their understanding was that sooner or later such persecution came to an end. They had no experience of the pathological extent of National Socialist anti-Semitism, and many found it impossible to believe that in Germany, of all countries – the 'safe harbour' that one Jewish deputy had referred to in 1871 – they were no longer safe. A third reason was that the National Socialist government made it increasingly hard to leave. Jews had to pay what amounted to an emigration tax which left all but the richest virtually penniless. All these combined to ensure that most Jews would remain: they had no choice.

From the very beginning, there were so-called 'wild' actions against Jews. These were mostly, but by no means exclusively, carried out by the SA. Jews and their property across Germany were physically attacked. Göring had designated the SA as an auxiliary police force, so it was clear that Jews could not hope for any legal redress. It has been argued that ordinary Germans were for the most part uninvolved in these actions, but this misses the point of them. They set the pattern for anti-Jewish persecution inside National Socialist Germany. There were to be no popular pogroms; anti-Jewish action was to be controlled by the government. Just as important, whether or not Germans approved of what was happening, the 'wild' actions habituated them to violence against the Jews. With rare exceptions, Jews would find that they could not rely on their 'Aryan' compatriots for help even in the most extreme circumstances. In March, the SA picketed the courthouse in Breslau in order to prevent the admission of Jewish lawyers and judges. Hitler attempted to bring these actions under control not, of course, because he had the slightest sympathy with the victims, but because he feared that the foreign Press would react negatively. Calling for 'blind discipline' from the SA, he nevertheless failed to prevent a continuation of the violence. A few days later, Jewish judges dealing with criminal cases in Bavaria were replaced. In late March, Hitler informed his entourage of his decision to order a nationwide boycott of Jewish shops ands businesses. A committee led by Julius Streicher, Gauleiter of Franconia and editor of *Der Stürmer*, would be placed in charge. The purpose of the boycott was clear. In several locations across Germany, anti-Semites had established boycotts of Jewish businesses; one on a nationwide basis would strike a blow at what Hans Günther had described as the economic preponderance of the Jews. It would also affirm that it was Hitler, and not the SA, who decided racial policy. In what was to become a pattern Hitler, having made the decision, took no further part in the action. The government would not be directly involved in the boycott. For official purposes, at least, it was Streicher's committee who would organise it. The official reason given for the boycott was that it was a protest against denunciations of the regime made to the foreign press by German Jews. It would begin on 1 April.

In fact the boycott was in important ways unsuccessful. For one thing, it lasted only a day. The main reason for this was the intervention of President Paul von Hindenburg. Though Hindenburg was sometimes described as senile at this time, in key areas he was still able to express an opinion. He remained a significant enough political force to see that his views counted. And although Hitler announced that the boycott would be resumed if the foreign press continued its anti-German stance, he had in fact been defeated. For a one-day boycott could only be a token gesture. On 1 April the Party newspaper *Völkischer Beobachter* ran a 'boycott' edition designed to encourage Germans to participate, alleging that evidence had been found that prominent Berlin Jews had visited foreign embassies in order to spread lies about anti-Jewish persecution.

The boycott's impact varied, inevitably, from place to place. In many places, such as Frankfurt, SA Stormtroopers ignored the instructions of local boycott committees and continued to take 'unauthorised' actions against Jews. In Kiel, a Jew was murdered when a mob forced its way into the police station where he was being held. In Berlin, however, the boycott was more disciplined. Even so, it ran into unanticipated problems. What, exactly, was a 'Jewish' business? Was it one merely owned by a Jew, or one which largely employed them? In the case of the four largest Berlin department stores, considered by the boycott committee to be Jewish and thus picketed by the SA, it was discovered to their embarrassment that they were mostly controlled by German or even foreign banks. They thus ended by having to be protected from the SA as 'Aryan' property. There were other problems. The mere fact that the boycott took place encouraged the more radical elements of the

Party, especially in the SA, to demand further action for which the government was not yet ready: it would be some time before Hitler would have the free hand he enjoyed after 1934. The boycott was extensively reported abroad and did serious damage to the reputation of the new government. Again, Hitler was not yet in a position to ignore the reaction of potential enemies abroad. From the Party's point of view, the most worrying aspect of the boycott was the lack of enthusiasm displayed by so many Germans. Crowds had gathered, but even observers favourable to the government agreed that this was more out of curiosity than anything else.

The boycott's failure certainly underlined the importance of taking racial policy away from the SA. It also showed that as yet most Germans were not prepared to participate actively in anti-Jewish activity; steps would have to be taken to ensure their willing co-operation. The problem of defining what exactly was a Jewish business was only part of a bigger issue: defining who was, and who was not, a Jew. The solution to all these problems, in Hitler's view, lay in legislation. After the failure of the 1923 Beer Hall Putsch, Hitler, always more pragmatic than most of his supporters, had been determined to achieve power by legal means. Since the boycott had proved unsuccessful, he would resort to legal methods too in order to solve the Jewish problem.

On 7 April 1933, Hitler signed the Law for the Restoration of a Professional Civil Service. The Enabling Act, Hitler rightly calculated, gave him sufficient authority to create this and virtually any other law. The new law, amongst other things, ensured the dismissal of civil servants who were not 'of Aryan descent', as well as those whose political records suggested that they might oppose the National Socialist revolution. President Hindenburg intervened again, winning exemptions for those who had served at the Front during the war; those who had lost a father or son, and those who had been in the civil service since the outbreak of the war in August 1914. These were relatively minor concessions. They did not alter the fact that for the first time since the creation of a united Germany, a definite end had been made to the principle that Jews who lived in Germany were Germans on the same basis as everyone else. Further laws followed. On 21 April, Jewish ritual slaughter of animals for food [*shechita*] was banned. The following day non-'Aryan' medical doctors, pharmacists and dentists were dismissed from hospitals and public health centres. This was followed by the Law Against the Over-Crowding of German Schools and Universities, which established a quota of 1.5% for non-'Aryan' admissions. In July came the Denaturalisation Law, which permitted the government to revoke the citizenship of anyone who had settled in Germany after 1918. Here the main targets were the *Ostjuden*, the Polish and Soviet Jews who had left their homes following the convulsions of the First World War and the Russian revolution and civil war. A law preventing Jews from owning land or even farming it came next. Shortly afterwards came the removal of non-'Aryan's from the various cultural groupings which now passed under the control of Josef Goebbels's propaganda ministry. Technically, none of this legislation could be described as 'racial', even though Germans usually referred to such decrees as *Rassengesetze* [racial laws]. For the purposes of this legislation, the government had defined 'non-Aryan' as anyone who had at least one Jewish grandparent. As yet, however, 'Jewish' was still a religious description, and not a racial one. Policy was still being improvised.

There were different ways to interpret the anti-Semitic legislation of 1933. It could be seen as a devastating series of blows against the long-established principle that Jews in Germany were equal citizens of the Reich. However, it was equally possible to believe that these laws had 'regularised' the conditions within which Jews could now hope for a relatively trouble-free existence. The new laws had removed their influence from the professions and from cultural life. Some Jews were able to hope that this would satisfy the National Socialists. In November 1933 a leading Jewish newspaper, the *Jüdische Rundschau*, concluded:

*If we look at the events of the past year, we must note that many German*

*Jews have lost the economic basis for their existence. Yet it appears from the announcements of the authorities that in future our economic existence will be guaranteed, though limited, by the new legal situation. In this light we can understand Dr Goebbels's remark that what needed to be solved concerning the Jewish question has been solved.*

This was optimistic in the extreme. In reality, of course, these laws had not been passed in order to secure basic rights for Germany's Jewish community. A few German Jews saw the situation with greater clarity. Victor Klemperer, a Jewish professor in Dresden who was married to an "Aryan" wife, recorded in his diary for 12 April,

*For the moment I am still safe. But as someone on the gallows, who has the rope around his neck, is still safe. At any moment a new "law" can kick away the steps on which I'm standing, and then I'm hanging.*

The legislation had emerged in order to render unnecessary the random attacks on Jews that had characterised the first weeks of the regime, and which had created a negative impression abroad. Legal measures against the Jews confirmed to the Party that the 'Jewish question' remained on the agenda. They also helped to confirm that Hitler, rather than the SA, would direct the pace and nature of anti-Jewish measures. To some extent, they represented the opening round in Hitler's battle with the SA, which would only be concluded in June 1934 with the Night of the Long Knives.

## The Nuremberg Laws

IT WAS CLEAR TO THOSE better acquainted with the National Socialist movement that the two years of relative calm which followed would not last indefinitely. The first sign came in May 1935 with the introduction of compulsory military service in Germany. The SS took the lead in demanding that Jews should not be permitted to serve. This was a first and ominous sign that the SS would now be increasingly involved in the formulation of racial policy, and not just its enforcement. In September 1935 new and much more stringent laws were announced at the annual Party rally. The laws were improvised and, to a great extent, designed to solve immediate political problems. They did not result from any long-term plan for Germany's Jews. The lack of any master-plan should not lead students, however, to conclude that there was no underlying direction to what was happening. It was clear that, however haphazard the process, the fundamental racial goal of the regime had not changed, and that there could be no long-term future for German Jews. How that goal was to be achieved, and what exactly might be meant by a Germany that was *Judenrein* – 'cleansed of Jews' – probably no one yet knew. Historian Mark Roseman describes National Socialist racial policy as a combination of constant energy and changing purpose. If historians find it difficult today to interpret, it was still more difficult for the Jews of Germany at the time. The American historian Peter Gay, whose family was finally to leave Germany in 1939, writes of the dilemma facing German Jews at this time:

> *The most formidable obstacle to fathoming things to come was the very insanity of the Hitlerian programme. 'It was all in* Mein Kampf" *has long been the litany of our detractors who, without an inkling of what uprooting ourselves meant and how hard it was to read the signals, reproached me or my parents for not having packed up on January 30, 1933 and left the country the next day. But Hitler's threats were so utterly implausible that we regarded them as unreliable guides to future conduct. They were literally incredible.*

Why was there renewed anti-Jewish activity in 1935? There were several reasons. One was the fact that during the early part of that year, some 10,000 Jews actually returned to Germany from abroad, encouraged by the fact that early excesses appeared to have ended. In addition, the numbers of those leaving Germany was beginning to fall. Clearly Jews were increasingly convinced that the worst was over. From the regime's viewpoint, this conviction had to be challenged. The Nuremberg Laws were also a response to the problems that had beset racial policy towards the Jews since 1933. How was it possible to remove Jews from the *Volk* community until there was a legally binding definition of a Jew? How could the various exemptions from such legislation as there were – for war veterans, for example – be rendered legally invalid?

Some idea of removing citizenship from Germany's Jews had existed since January 1933, when the Ministry of the Interior had set up a committee on population and racial policy. German-'Aryan' marriages had also long been under scrutiny. In July 1935 the Justice Ministry submitted a proposal to ban such marriages. It is clear, therefore, that whatever role Hitler personally played in the creation of the Nuremberg laws, these topics were already the object of serious discussion within the bureaucracy. The major impetus for the passing of the laws in September was probably Hitler's need, following the Night of the Long Knives the previous summer, to make clear to his supporters that the Party remained in charge of racial policy. In his speech on the first day of the Party rally in September, Hitler emphasised that the Party would not be held back by the bureaucracy. This was an irony, granted that the bureaucrats had been taking the lead in renewing discussion about policy. According to historian Saul Friedländer, there had been growing discontent in the lower ranks of the Party about the lack of pace in racial policy and especially in policy directed against the Jews. With the Nuremberg laws, Hitler was seen to regain the initiative. The original plan had been for Hitler to announce new legislation forbidding Jews to fly the swastika flag on the last day of the rally. With only hours to go, Hitler appears to have decided that this would make an unimpressive announcement: Jews, after all, were hardly likely to hoist swastika flags in any case. The Interior minister, Wilhelm Frick, had long been contemplating the banning of German-'Aryan' marriages, as had the Reich Medical Chief, Gerhard Wagner. At some stage Hitler instructed Frick to produce a law to this effect. To do this would also require, for the first time, a clear and unambiguous definition of what exactly a Jew was in law.

The new laws were drafted, only the night before the speech was due, by officials from the Justice Department. They had been urgently summoned to Nuremberg by the *Führer*. There was another irony in this: one of them was Bernhard Lösener, in charge of Section I of the Interior Ministry, which had charge of Jewish legislation. Lösener had become disenchanted with the NSDAP and had persistently attempted to reduce the impact of legislation against the Jews. Now he attempted to minimise the number of people who would be affected by the new laws. This meant attempting to convince Hitler that only full Jews should be included, and not the half or quarter-Jewish *Mischlinge*. Hitler, however, initially refused this draft and insisted that a harsher version be prepared. He also demanded the creation of a Reich Citizenship Law, also to be announced the following day. By the time Hitler actually made the speech on 15 September, however, he had changed his mind, and the law governing 'Aryan'-German unions was to apply only to full Jews.

The two new laws were the Law for the Protection of German Blood and German Honour, and the Reich Citizenship Law. Under the first, marriages and sexual relations between 'Aryans' and full Jews were forbidden. To help ensure this, one paragraph made it illegal for Jews to employ German domestic servants under the age of forty-five. The Citizenship Law was vaguer. Jews did not, in theory, lose their status as German citizens, but were unable to aspire to a new and higher form of citizenship which belonged to 'Aryans' only, but which was not defined. When Hitler announced these laws to a specially convened session of the Reichstag, however, he omitted the crucial sentence about the new blood law applying only to full Jews. This meant that it still remained unclear who was to be affected by the Nuremberg laws. Debate on this issue continued well after September 1935. Lösener continued to argue for a 'soft' interpretation, but Wagner argued that a Jew meant someone with at least one Jewish grandparent. On occasion, he argued that even one Jewish great-grandparent should be enough to define a person as Jewish. Lösener pointed out that such a strict definition would be bound to turn many people against the regime who at the moment were not opposed to it; he also argued that a person of one-eighth Jewish ancestry was seven-eighths German. Finally a supplementary law was published in November 1935. A full or three-quarter Jew – that is, a person with four or three Jewish grandparents – was fully subject to the Nuremberg laws. A half-Jew, on the other hand, would only be considered Jewish if she or he practised Judaism; was married to a Jew; or was the child of a marriage with one Jewish partner, or was the result of an illegal 'Aryan'-German union. The inclusion of a religious element made nonsense of the theory that it was blood which made the Jew, but this does not appear to have occurred to anyone either then or later. It was estimated that half a million people could now be defined as Jews; an additional 300,000 could be defined as *Mischlinge*. The latter were 'safe' for the moment. But an announcement made in 1936 stressed that the solution to the *Mischling* question was the disappearance of the *Mischling* 'race' altogether. This – provided the Nuremberg laws could be enforced – would happen within one or two generations at the most.

How did Jews react to the Nuremberg Laws? Victor Klemperer recorded, 'I have the impression that an explosion is imminent. I am reckoning on a pogrom; the ghetto; money and house to be taken away, anything Rather. I am reckoning on nothing. I wait gloomy and helpless.'

But once again, there was no explosion. The relative calm was in part due to the need to placate foreign opinion. The Olympic Games of 1936 were a golden opportunity for the regime to show itself to advantage, and this meant a reduction in overt anti-Jewish actions. Hitler ordered anti-Jewish signs to be removed from the region round Garmisch-Partenkirchen, where the Winter Olympics would be held, and this example was followed in Berlin when the main Games took place in August 1936. This was not the only impact that the XI Olympiad had on racial life in Germany: Romani camps near Berlin were emptied and their inhabitants moved to closed camps elsewhere; and the police were instructed that the laws against homosexuality were not to be enforced in the case of foreign visitors.

What conclusions can be drawn from the passing of the Nuremberg laws? One is that the whole episode was very typical of National Socialist racial policy in general, and Hitler's role in it in particular. The passing of the laws was the product of particular and immediate circumstances, rather than the specific outcome of a long-term plan. The legislation had its origins, however, in discussions held over a long period within the bureaucracy, so that when action was needed there were officials ready to act. The episode also showed that, even within a single government department, there could be diametrically opposed views on the form which policy should take, even if there was agreement on the larger objective. There was also conflict between agencies. Hitler's intervention was simultaneously decisive and vacillating. There would be more examples of all this in the years ahead.

The laws passed in 1935 brought little comfort to the most radical elements in the NSDAP. Though they had finally legally defined a Jew, the laws had done nothing to remove Jews from the national community. They allowed Jews to hope, just as some had done after the legislation of 1933, that it might now be possible to live relatively unmolested. This view received encouragement from an interview given by Hitler to a foreign newspaper, in which he stated that attacks on Jews would cease provided the Jews themselves did not create any further provocations. The Nuremberg laws also offered no rapid solution to the *Mischling* question. Radical members of the Party drew some comfort from the disenfranchising of Jews in November 1935, which followed the Reich Citizenship Law, and the dismissal of civil servants hitherto protected by their status as war veterans. A second supplementary law banned Jewish lawyers, teachers and doctors from state service, a move followed in 1938 by the banning of all Jewish professionals. These measures were accompanied by 'private', or non-governmental actions against Jews at all levels of society. Jews had their insurance policies terminated.

Most private clubs and associations also expelled Jewish members; books by Jewish authors were purged from schools and libraries. Local by-laws banned Jews from swimming-pools, park benches, theatres, cinemas and some classes of public transport. Jews were forbidden to hold hunting licenses, to practice as veterinarians, to work as currency-dealers, to deal in livestock, to work as construction engineers. After 1937 even 'Aryans' married to Jews were no longer allowed to fly the national flag or give the Hitler greeting. Streets named after prominent Jews were renamed. In 1939, all Jews had to add the names 'Israel' or 'Sara' to their own, and their passports and identification papers were stamped with the letter 'J'. After the *Anschluß* of March 1938, of course, all anti-Jewish legislation was applied to Austrian Jews as well.

Increasingly, Jews were becoming both socially and economically marginalised. 1938 saw a drive to 'Aryanise' the economy, by the simple means of forcibly transferring Jewish businesses and property to non-Jewish hands. In 1933, according to Michael Burleigh, there had been about 50,000 Jewish-owned businesses in Germany. By April 1938 there were only 32,532. A year later, 15,000 of these businesses had been liquidated and 17,000 had been 'Aryanised' or were in the process of being so. All assets in excess of RM 50,000 had to be registered with the authorities, preparing the way for discriminatory taxation. By the spring of 1938, 21% of the Jewish population was dependent on Jewish charities, despite the upturn in the German economy as a whole.

In addition, the regime encouraged the now accelerating pace of Jewish emigration. The principal obstacle to Jewish emigration from Germany continued to be the German government itself, which still insisted that German Jews, and those living abroad, should effectively pay in hard currency for the right to leave. An international gathering at Evian in August 1938 unsuccessfully attempted to find some solution to this problem. German representatives refused to move on this issue: it was also clear, however, that foreign governments were still unwilling to accept large numbers of Jews, even if the problem had been solved. Despite this, emigration remained the ideal solution in the eyes of the regime. The SS gave encouragement to Jewish organisations which promoted the idea of emigration to Palestine and other countries, whilst harassing those that still sought some degree of assimilation.

Although the SS did not yet dominate racial policy, it was now consciously preparing to do so, having established a section in 1936, – under Adolf Eichmann – specifically with this objective in mind. The 1939 census for the first time contained 'supplementary' questions on racial origin, allowing the SD, the SS security service, to compile a detailed card-index on all Jews within Greater Germany. This would greatly facilitate the work of the SS in the years ahead. Jews found guilty of breaking the Nuremberg laws were transferred, after completion of a jail sentence, to the concentration camps run by the SS.

## The Night of Broken Glass

IT WAS THE EVENTS OF NOVEMBER 1938, however, which convinced many that there could be no future for Jews in National Socialist Germany. In March 1938, the Polish government, not much less anti-Semitic than the German one, declared its intention to annul the citizenship of Polish Jews living in Germany. Since these Ostjuden had already been deprived of German citizenship, the regime was faced with the prospect of having several thousand stateless Jews on its hands. The German government reacted by simply rounding up as many of them as it could, and dumping them across the Polish frontier. Since the Poles refused to admit them, they ended up camped in appalling conditions in the no-man's-land between the two countries. Amongst them were the parents of one Herzl [Herschel] Grynszpan. Grynszpan, born in Hanover, was a seventeen-year-old living in Paris whilst he waited to emigrate to Palestine. After receiving news of his parents' plight, he bought a cheap revolver on 7 November and made his way to the German embassy. There he fatally shot a German diplomat, Ernst vom Rath. A note to his mother, found in his pocket, made it clear that the attack was a direct retaliation for the fate of the Polish Jews expelled from Germany. Vom Rath died on 9 November, coincidentally the anniversary of the Beer Hall Putsch, when most of the leading figures in the NSDAP were in Munich to commemorate the failed uprising of 1923.

Propaganda minister Josef Goebbels took the lead. It is clear that he spoke with Hitler at length about the appropriate response to events in Paris. His diary recorded:

*Big [anti-Jewish] demonstrations in Kassel and Dessau, synagogues set on fire and buildings demolished. The death of the German diplomat vom Rath is reported in the afternoon. But now the goose is cooked. I go to the Party reception in the Old Town Hall. Colossal activity. I brief the Führer about the matter. He orders: Let the demonstrations go on. Withdraw the police. The Jews must for once feel the people's anger. That is right.*

Hitler then left the Town Hall, leaving Goebbels to make a speech to the assembled Party functionaries, in which he informed them, 'The *Führer* has decided that demonstrations should not be prepared or organised by the Party, but insofar as they erupt spontaneously, they are not to be hampered.' It was clear, therefore, that Goebbels received his authority from Hitler, and that there is no truth whatever in assertions by Holocaust deniers that Hitler either knew nothing about the events or that he disapproved of them. Instructions from Heinrich Müller, head of Section II of Sipo, the Security Police, and from Heydrich, head of the SD, were then issued to Germany's police officials. Müller warned them of what was to happen, and made it clear that, whilst they were not to interfere in the demonstrations, they must take steps to prevent looting. They were also to prepare for the arrest of 20 – 30,000 Jews. The number of Jews to be arrested had been specified by Hitler during his meeting with Goebbels. Heydrich's orders directed police and security agencies to take only such steps to protect Jewish lives and property as were necessary to prevent fires, for example, from spreading to German property, and reiterated the prohibition on looting. Foreigners were not to be assaulted, even if they were Jewish. There is evidence to suggest that Heinrich Himmler, in overall charge of the German police, had met with Hitler before these orders were sent.

The result was a pogrom of a type and intensity that had not been experienced in Germany since the Middle Ages. Contrary to the claims of the regime, the anti-Jewish actions which flared across Germany were neither initiated nor for the most part carried out by ordinary citizens. However, the pogrom was carried out in full public view, and only in rare circumstances did 'ordinary' Germans intervene. In part this was due to intimidation. The regime had destroyed the institutions which might have offered organised resistance, and made open opposition extremely dangerous. In addition, years of anti-Semitic legislation and propaganda, as well as the common sight of physical assaults carried out on Jews, had led to reluctance to protest such actions. Jews had already become such marginal figures in Germany that it may have seemed not worth taking the risk involved in helping them; perhaps it never occurred to many Germans to do so.

By the early morning of 10 November 1938, perhaps 500 synagogues had been burned, destroyed or badly damaged. The great majority of those Jewish shops still in business had also been attacked, and many totally destroyed. At least 91 Jews had been murdered; shot, beaten, stabbed, drowned or driven to suicide. Thousands more were in custody, where they would experience varying degrees of humiliation and ill-treatment. A rabbi in Düsseldorf, Max Eschenbacher, indicates what the night had been like:

*I was seized by an SA man, and dragged about in a great arc in front of the house. I was then thrown into the entrance of the building. Then the district leader came and said, 'I am taking you into protective custody'. The march to police headquarters began. A squad of SA men was before us. Then me, escorted by two of them. Then again, a squad of SA people. The whole way they sang in unison, 'Revenge for Paris! Down with the*

*Jews!' Passers by, who encountered us on the streets also shouted, 'Revenge for Paris! Down with the Jews!*

Eschenbacher was held in custody for twelve days before being released. Several people he knew had died. His synagogue had been set on fire by a mob clearly not just composed of the SA: it included local councillors and even physicians from the municipal hospital.

The Night of Broken Glass – or, as the regime sarcastically called it, *Reichskristallnacht* – marked a true turning-point in National Socialist policy towards the Jews. As Goebbels recorded, 'The whole question has now been taken a good step further'. It was now possible to effect measures which had not been considered practical. On 12 November, Göring chaired a meeting designed to punish the Jewish community still further for their alleged responsibility, not only for the assassination of vom Rath, but for the pogrom itself. A total of RM 1 billion was to be extracted as a form of collective fine; all Jews were to pay a tax worth 25% of their assets, to be collected in instalments. In addition, Jews were to pay the cost of repairing the damage caused on the nights of 9/10 November, so that 'Aryan' insurance companies should not have to suffer the cost of reconstruction. Any insurance money claimed by Jews was to be confiscated. A decree 'for the Exclusion of Jews from German Economic Life' was also agreed, which effectively closed more Jewish businesses and further restricted Jewish employment. Göring's earlier anxieties about the impact of anti-Jewish legislation on the long-term prospects for the economy had now clearly been swept away. This was a ruthless search for Jewish assets in the face of a deteriorating international situation, with war clearly imminent. A further decree in December permitted Jews to pass goods and assets, including jewellery and art works, only to the State, rather than to family members. That same month, Jews were forbidden to drive motor cars: it apparently gave offence to 'Aryans' that Jews were using motorways that had been built with German labour. Jews were also forbidden to enter the government district of central

Berlin. In February 1939, Jews had to surrender all precious metals to the government.

Victor Klemperer recorded, 'These few [Germans], sympathising and in despair, are isolated, and they too are afraid. The developments of the last few days have at least rid us of inner uncertainty: there is no longer any choice: we must leave'. But as we have seen, this was extremely difficult. Academics such as Klemperer were not needed by countries that might have been willing to accept farmers, skilled craftsmen or labourers. Few German Jews fitted this profile. Age also counted against them: 35% of German Jews were over the age of fifty. In addition, Germany was not the only country where anti-Semitism was encouraging Jews to leave: Poland, Romania, the Baltic states and Hungary all saw large numbers of Jews attempting to emigrate. From this perspective, German Jews appeared least financially deserving of support. Above all, the impact of the Depression, and fear of an anti-Jewish backlash in their own countries, inhibited foreign governments from extending refuge to the Jews of Germany. The majority of Germany's Jews – including Victor Klemperer – would still be there when, on 1 September, German troops crossed the frontier into Poland and the Second World War began. Few would survive until its end.

| Year | Number of emigrants | Total since 1933 |
| --- | --- | --- |
| 1933 | 37,000 | 37,000 |
| 1934 | 23,000 | 60,000 |
| 1935 | 21,000 | 81,000 |
| 1936 | 25,000 | 106,000 |
| 1937 | 23,000 | 129,000 |
| 1938 | 25,000 | 149,000 |

TABLE I: *Jewish emigration from Germany: 1933–1938*

## Questions

- ❏ Why did so few Jews leave Germany between 1933 and 1939?
- ❏ In what ways, and to what extent, were the Nuremberg laws an important development in policy towards the Jews?
- ❏ How far was the Night of Broken Glass a turning-point in National Socialist racial policy?

.

# Chapter 4: In What Ways Was A Racial Community Created between 1933 and 1939?

Dɪᴅ Nᴀᴛɪᴏɴᴀʟ Sᴏᴄɪᴀʟɪsᴍ sᴜᴄᴄᴇᴇᴅ in creating the racial utopia that theorists had dreamed of since the formation of the NSDAP in 1919? The evolution of policy towards the Jews was examined in Chapter 3, but what of the other minority groups within Germany? This chapter examines who these groups were and how the regime perceived them, as well as how policy towards them evolved in the years before 1939.

Several minority groups attracted attention from the National Socialist medical-legal hierarchy. The *Erbkranke*, or 'hereditarily ill', were one of the first targets of the National Socialist obsession with biology. This category included those with chronic or inherited mental illness or handicap. The term also covered some social categories, rather than racial or biological ones, but this was always a rather narrow distinction in National Socialist Germany.

Homosexuality was also established quite quickly as a social-biological problem, with the implication that perhaps a cure could be found or, failing this, some solution to the problem. As we have already seen there was always a tendency, in National Socialist Germany, for the most radical solution to become the one finally adopted. Other groups were regarded with equal suspicion. These included the small population of black Germans, both those from Germany's former African colonies and others of mixed race. The **Sorb** population of east-central Germany was seen as problematic; so was the more substantial **Sinti** and **Roma** population, popularly known as 'Gypsies'. There could clearly be no case, in the eyes of the National Socialist regime, for accepting the presence of such distinctive groups of racial inferiors within the German heartland.

Efforts to reduce or eliminate the threat posed by such groups were necessarily balanced by the desire to maximise the possibility of enlarging and improving Germany's Nordic or Aryan stock. Abortion was already illegal, but after 1933 the penalty was increased to two years' imprisonment. During the war, abortion carried the death penalty when practised on Aryan mothers. Naturally, there was no such prohibition on abortion for those deemed racially or hereditarily inferior. Loans were provided for young married couples, with 25% being cancelled upon the birth of a child. In some cities, parents with large numbers of children were entitled to reduction in rent and the cost of domestic utilities. Famously, from 1938, women who produced large numbers of babies were decorated with the Honour Cross of the German Mother. Attempts were made to reduce the stigma of unmarried motherhood. Heinrich Himmler set up what were known as _Lebensbornheime_ – Well of Life homes – where unmarried mothers could receive free ante- and post-natal care; after 1939 they also functioned as adoption centres for Polish and other children thought fit for Germanisation. None of this actually had much effect on the birthrate, which if anything declined during the National Socialist period. So in a further attempt to improve Germany's racial balance, large numbers of ethnic Germans were re-settled within the Reich or its incorporated territories. Other groups were deported to make room for them. 'Germanisation' was also initiated once the war had begun, particularly in the former Czech territories and in Poland, and thousands of 'racially suitable' children were abducted and transferred to German families.

## 'Life Unworthy of Life'

THERE WAS NOTHING SPECIFICALLY NATIONAL SOCIALIST, or peculiarly German, about attitudes towards those who suffered from mental or physical handicap, especially where these were known or thought to be hereditary. Many countries, including Great Britain and the United States, had long expressed anxiety about the drain on resources that these individuals represented. This was not merely a question of finance, though propaganda in most Western countries emphasised that the cost of keeping alive hordes of what were described as 'idiots' was equal to, or greater than, the cost of providing support to deserving families. In Germany things went further but not, to start with, that much further. In July 1933 the Reichstag passed a Law for the Prevention of Hereditarily Diseased Offspring, which came into force the following year. It mandated compulsory sterilisation for a number of categories of illness, including alcoholism. This meant that while 'racial' victims of the regime survived some years of suffering social and legal persecution, the full weight of physical terror descended on the handicapped from the outset. Hereditary Health Courts decided who should be sterilised. Most of the early victims of this legislation were not in fact hereditarily ill, even using the vague definition that the Hereditary Health Courts employed, but were classified as 'asocial' or 'community aliens'.

Further laws followed, specifically targeting those who were designated as 'habitual criminals'. A law concerning these was passed in December 1933, permitting the sterilisation of those found members of this group deemed to be dangerous: they might suffer castration. Even juvenile delinquents might be subjected to this penalty, under a law on delinquency adopted in January 1937.

Just as the Nuremberg laws of 1935 marked a significant change in the persecution of the Jews, so the same year saw a growing radicalisation of policy towards those regarded as outside the **Volksgemeinschaft**. The Law on the Prevention of Hereditarily Diseased Offspring was amended, permitting compulsory abortion of foetuses belonging to women categorised as hereditarily ill. A second piece of legislation, the Law for the Preservation of the German People's Health, was passed in October 1935. From now on, there would be compulsory registration of those outside the *Volksgemeinschaft,* which included the hereditarily ill and those of 'lesser racial value'. Registration was always, in National Socialist Germany, potentially dangerous and often lethal. In an age before computers, the automated card-index systems of such agencies as the SS and the SD, imported in 1936 from the American company IBM, were the next best thing. They were able to record vast amounts of data, retrievable at will. Through one law or another, much of the German population could be registered. The two censuses held during the National Socialist period, in 1933 and 1939, were also of particular value in this respect. Once registered , people could be classified. For groups such as the hereditarily ill and the Sinti and Roma, classification would all too often be only the preliminary to murder. The law also mandated that all those wishing to marry must first obtain a certificate of fitness to do so.

In addition, the Propaganda Ministry encouraged the production of a number of films, both features and documentaries, to increase public awareness of the problem. Such films depicted the mentally ill in graphic ways. In many of them, mental illness was depicted as closely connected with, if not identical to, criminality. At a time of economic depression, the cost of keeping such people alive in 'idyllic' surroundings was also made explicit. Misleading statistics exaggerated not only the number of hereditarily ill people in Germany, but also falsely suggested that their birth-rate exceeded that of the 'normal' population.

Propaganda was also aimed at the young. Mathematical problems in school posed such problems as:

*The construction of a lunatic asylum costs 6 million Reichsmark [RM]. How many houses at 15,000 RM each could have been built for the same money?*

Or:

*To keep a mentally ill person costs approximately 4 RM a day; a cripple 5.50 RM; a criminal 3.30 RM. Many civil servants receive only 4RM per day; white-collar employees barely 3.50 RM; unskilled workers not even 2 RM per head for their families. (Illustrate these figures with a diagram).*

The most urgent requirement was to prevent the further breeding of these undesirables. The medical profession became heavily implicated in the resultant programme of sterilisation, which was initiated in 1935. The operation was run by a special organisation located at Tiergartenstraße 4 in Berlin, and which therefore became known as *Aktion T-4*.

Hitler himself, according to his personal physician Karl Brandt, stated that

*if a war should break out he would take up the euthanasia issue and implement it, because [he] was of the opinion that such a problem would be easier and smoother to carry out in wartime since the public resistance one could expect from the churches would not play such a prominent role amidst the events of wartime as it otherwise would.' As we shall see, the euthanasia policy was not the only one that it was believed could be carried out far more easily in wartime conditions.*

## Homosexuality

UNLIKE MUCH OF Europe, male homosexual activity had not always been illegal in all parts of Germany. Homosexual acts between consenting males had been decriminalised in several German states in the course of the nineteenth century, the result of the spread of Enlightenment ideals. The exception was **Prussia**, by far the largest of the German states. Article 175 of the Prussian law code asserted that such activity would be punished with imprisonment. When Germany was united in 1871, this part of the Prussian legal code was extended to the rest of Germany. Apart from the legal consequences for homosexual activity, there was a good deal of social disapproval. An accusation could ruin even the most prominent individual, as several high-profile cases in the **Second Reich** demonstrated. Philip von Eulenburg, one of the closest friends of the emperor Wilhelm II, had been disgraced by a homosexual scandal in 1907, even though no proof had ever been produced of what former chancellor Bernhard von Bülow described as his 'lack of erotic integrity'.

It is often assumed that the Weimar government either repealed or softened Article 175. In fact, it did neither. It was true, however, that in some areas – notably Berlin – the police became somewhat more tolerant, even though this could never be wholly relied on. Changes in attitudes towards homosexuals may have been the result of a more tolerant public opinion, at least in some of the big cities. If so, this change may have been partly due to the activities of social scientists such as Magnus Hirschfeld, whose Institute of Sexual Science had opened in 1919 during the first, liberal phase of the Weimar Republic. Its publications had a considerable effect on public perception of sexual conditions. So too did the work of Sigmund Freud, working in Vienna until 1938. His psychoanalytical theories, so shocking when they were first published at the turn of the century, had become part of mainstream thinking thirty years later. In 1930 Freud was awarded the Goethe Prize, one of Germany's most prestigious literary awards. He was perfectly clear that homosexuality was not an illness, and still less a crime.

But such views did not reflect, and certainly did not initiate, any change in the law. On the contrary, traditionalists worried that 'perverts' were taking advantage of a change in the moral climate to seduce the young. In 1925 an amendment to the law was proposed which would have increased the penalties for homosexual activity.

*National Socialist Racial Policy*

Although this was defeated in the Reichstag in 1929, by a coalition of left-wing and liberal parties, it suggested that there was a strong reaction against the prevailing liberalism which would rapidly be exploited by the National Socialists when they came to power in 1933.

What exactly were the National Socialist objections to homosexuality? After all, the SA leader Ernst Röhm was only the most prominent of several leading Party members who were homosexuals. Though this was certainly known to Hitler, it did not seem to have affected their relationship. One reason was probably that Hitler liked his followers to have what he called 'a flaw in the weave'. By this he meant that they should have some weakness; it made it easier for him to bring them to heel if necessary. Another reason for Hitler's apparent indifference to homosexuality within the NSDAP was that any action on his part would only increase the political vulnerability he felt on the issue. Both communists and socialists were not above exploiting it for party political purposes. It should have been obvious to them that their true interest was in supporting homosexuals, most of whom were understandably anti-National Socialist. As so often, however, organisations such as the **SPD** and **KPD** seem to have found it impossible to work with other groups against a common enemy. Instead they preferred to maintain that the working-class was essentially heterosexual and thus that homosexuality was a conservative or middle-class phenomenon. Headlines in the SPD newspaper *Münchener Post*, for example, claiming that there was a 'brotherhood of nancy-boys in the **Brown House**' could only have alienated homosexuals of whatever political orientation.

For this reason, then, Hitler felt obliged to ignore, if not condone, Röhm's activities. This changed on 30 June 1934, on the so-called Night of the Long Knives. On that day Röhm and a number of other SA leaders were arrested and summarily executed. At least one of them, Breslau SA leader Eduard Heines, was discovered in bed with a young man. Afterwards, it became convenient for the

National Socialist leadership to claim that the purge, at last in part, had been a successful attempt by Hitler to 'clean up' the NSDAP. Opponents of the regime were depressed to discover that this apparent attack on 'perversion' within his own party was popular even with those who regarded themselves as opposed to National Socialism.

The more significant campaign against homosexuality was led by Heinrich Himmler, *Reichsführer-SS* and Head of the German Police. Himmler claimed, without much evidence, that there were two million homosexual men in Germany. He saw them principally as a biological resource that refused to procreate. Germany had lost a similar number of men in the World War and this meant that four million males either could not or would not reproduce. This was a luxury that no country could afford, especially a country such as Germany, which would shortly be involved in military action to reshape a continent. Sexuality was no longer a private matter. Nor was it enough simply to stop homosexuals from being homosexuals. The real benefit to the racial community would come when they had decisively changed their sexual orientation and entered the world of procreation.

Paragraph 175 was amended in 1935 and now covered all and any acts of 'criminal indecency' between males. This resulted in a substantial increase in prosecutions of homosexuals. Within the SS itself homosexuality became, in practice, a capital offence. In wider German society, convicted homosexuals – particularly those also suspected of political deviance – were usually sent to concentration camps upon completion of their sentence. It was here that they were marked with the pink triangle that was to become an icon of the post-war gay sub-culture. Inmates agreed that homosexuals were particularly harshly treated in the camps. In some cases, efforts were made to 're-educate' them into changing their sexual orientation; mostly, of course, without success. This was another demonstration of the fact that for all their concern on 'racial-hygienic' grounds, the National Socialists fundamentally misunderstood

*National Socialist Racial Policy*

homosexuality, seeing it primarily as a symptom of personal moral degeneracy. And Himmler's preferred solution within the SS – that homosexuals be put to death – was based on another and characteristic misunderstanding. This was that the Iron Age bodies that turned up in northern Europe's peat bogs from time to time were those of executed homosexuals. Modern archaeologists are almost unanimous in concluding that they are in fact the bodies of sacrificial victims, and that there is no evidence whatever that they were killed because of their sexual orientation.

Whether the National Socialists misunderstood homosexuality or not, the principal effect of the persecution was to drive homosexual activity underground, rather than to eliminate it. Men went to extraordinary lengths to meet like-minded companions, never sure that they were not being tracked by the Gestapo or other police agencies, which devoted a disproportionate amount of time to the pursuit and subsequent prosecution of homosexuality.

Why were female homosexuals – lesbians – not pursued with equal severity? It most certainly was not the case, as some have alleged, that the 'naïve' National Socialists did not believe that such a thing existed. They knew better than that. The reason was that they thought that it would in practice be difficult to obtain convictions in lesbian cases. It was often difficult to do so even in the case of men since, at least in theory, it was necessary to catch both parties *in flagrante*. In the case of women, where social custom permitted a good deal of physical contact, it would be all but impossible. However, lesbianism could be, and sometimes was, taken into account if an individual was under investigation.

## Sorbs

THE SORBS WERE MUCH LESS OF A PROBLEM. A small group of Slavic origin, the Sorbs had lived in the Lausitz area of eastern Germany for many centuries. They had extensively intermingled with the local German population, and there was some doubt as to how far they really retained their Slavic character. For that matter, the SD did not even know how many Sorbs there were. A 1940 survey conducted in Upper Lausitz counted only 3,500 of them, though the SD was certain that there were at least four times as many, and concluded that many had concealed their racial identity. If true, this was unsurprising. Sorb-language newspapers and political associations had been closed in 1937. Sorb teachers and clergy were forcibly transferred from the Lausitz area. However, since only language and costume appeared to differentiate the Sorb from the German, racial experts concluded that no further radical measures were necessary. Sorb culture need not be publicly denigrated: indeed, it would be better if its existence were not mentioned at all. 'Peaceful cultural penetration' should aim to absorb the Sorbs, and this meant sending Sorb children to German-speaking kindergartens and schools, employing Sorb women as domestic servants in German households, and inducting Sorb men into the army or other National Socialist formations. Germanisation would be the key to the ultimate disappearance of the Sorbs.

## 'Black' Germans

THERE WERE RELATIVELY few black people in Germany in the 1930s: probably not more than a few thousand altogether. The majority had arrived from Germany's pre-war colonies in Africa – Cameroun, and what are now Tanzania and Namibia. Rarely fully accepted by white society, they were subject to the sort of racial discrimination that was common in western societies until very recently. The memoirs of Hans-Jürgen Massaquoi, whose mother was German and whose father was Liberian, describe how he was racially abused at school by literally hundreds of boys. However, the small number of black people, and the fact that they were scattered across Germany's big industrial cities, meant that they were not generally perceived as a threat by the National Socialist regime. This was provided, of course, that they kept their hands off German women. Massaquoi recorded how, during the war, he was arrested on his way home by the SD. The arresting agent stated his belief that Massasquoi had been 'on the prowl for defenceless women'. It was only because a local policeman vouched for his character that Massaquoi was released. Although the Nuremberg Laws of 1935 did not specifically mention black people, most authorities took it for granted that their provisions also applied to intermarriage between blacks and Germans. A circular issued by the Reich and Prussian ministry of the interior in November 1935 instructed registry offices not to issue 'certificates of fitness to marry' in the event of unions where offspring 'deleterious to German blood' could be anticipated. This applied to Jews, Sinti and Roma; it also applied to 'Negroes and their bastards'.

For most Germans, it went without saying that black people were both racially and culturally inferior. Like most Europeans of the time, Hitler believed that Africa had no civilisation or culture of its own, and no history before the arrival of Europeans. He strongly objected to the importation into Germany of such black culture as there was, whether from Africa or from the United States. He was dismayed by the popularity of jazz, which National Socialists almost invariably referred to as 'nigger music' and which was largely outlawed during the Third Reich. It must be doubted that Adolf Hitler was ever in the presence of a black person of any nationality for very long. There is, however, no truth in the enduring myth that Hitler was incensed by the victories of Jesse Owens, the African American athlete who won five gold medals at the Berlin Olympic Games of 1936, and, refusing to meet him, stormed out of the stadium. Hitler would have agreed with the German teacher who told his class, 'For a German runner to lose to one of these half-civilised people from America, is no more a disgrace than losing to a horse. Everybody knows that a horse is physically superior but mentally inferior: the same is true for these Hottentots from America.'

During the Second World War, Germans encountered French, British and American soldiers of African origin. The regime made extensive propaganda of the employment by the allies of such racially inferior elements. When black soldiers were captured, they were usually held in segregated camps. It should be pointed out that in the case of African Americans this was frequently at the request, or with the agreement, of white prisoners: the United States armed forces would remain segregated until 1950. There were also atrocities against black prisoners. During the campaign in France of 1940 French African soldiers were sometimes shot on the spot; in an incident in Belgium in December 1944, eleven African American prisoners were tortured and then murdered by *Waffen-SS* troops. However, there was no systematic massacre of captured black combatants, in striking contrast to the treatment of prisoners of war on the Eastern front. As many as three million Soviet prisoners may have died in German captivity, mostly from starvation, brutal ill-treatment and random executions. On the whole, National Socialist policies towards people of African descent were not notably different from those practised by Germany's enemies. This accurately reflected the pervasive anti-black feeling of the time.

However, an even smaller minority of black Germans did experience the full impact of National Socialist racial policy. These were the so-called '**Rhineland bastards**', the offspring of German women and French African soldiers who had been in occupation of the Rhineland after the First World War. Such unions may have been inevitable, but a large number of Germans saw them as shameful and totally unacceptable. Even during the Weimar republic there had been calls to 'do something' about these children. Writing in 1927, racial theorist Hans Günther condemned France for 'giving the Negro, through the granting of civil rights and officer's rank, an influence whose full results we cannot yet see. For Germany, the French domination involves the "Black Shame" – the attacks by Africans on white women in the occupied territory'. For people like Günther, it was self-evident that no white woman would have voluntarily consorted with a black man. He cited with approval the American author Lothtrop Stoddard, whose influential book *The Rising Tide of Color Against White World Supremacy* had been published in 1920. According to Stoddard,

*The more primitive a type is, the more prepotent [powerful] it is. This is why crossings with the negro are uniformly fatal. Whites, Amerindians, or Asiatics - all are alike vanquished by the invincible prepotency of the more primitive, generalized, and lower negro blood.*

This combination – of national humiliation following military defeat, and a widespread belief that cohabitation with blacks was 'fatal' to other races – explains why a few hundred dual-heritage children were seen as such a threat by successive German regimes. Once the National Socialists were in power, they lost no time in devising a policy to remove this threat for good. The announcement was made by Walther Darré, the new minister for food and agriculture, who would soon take over the RuSHA. According to Darré,

*It is essential to exterminate the leftovers from the black Shame on the Rhine. These mulatto [mixed-race] children were created either through rape or by white mothers who were whores. In any case, there exists not the slightest obligation towards these racially foreign offspring. About fourteen years have elapsed in the meantime; those mulattoes who are still alive will now be entering the age of puberty. That doesn't leave time for long discussions. Let France and other nations deal with their race questions the way they want. For us there is only one solution, extermination of all that is foreign, especially those that through violence and lack of morality have created this danger. Thus, as a Rhinelander, I demand the sterilisation of all mulattoes with whom we were saddled by the black Shame of the Rhine.*

Darré was not, in fact, a Rhinelander, though he had attended university there. Instead, like many of the leading racial policy-makers of the Third Reich, he did not even come from Germany; he had been born in Argentina. Nonetheless, his demands were rapidly met. Sterilisation, rather than physical extermination, was the preferred – or at least, initial – solution to the so-called Rhineland shame. Several hundred young adults of mixed race were sterilised during the 1930s This was usually undertaken by general hospitals; the medical profession in general raising no objection to the forcible sterilisation of perfectly healthy adolescents. Once sterilised, some were let go; others ended in concentration camps or, during the war, were used as slave labour. No one knows how many died as a result of racial policy in this area.

# The Sinti and Roma

ONE RACIAL GROUP IDENTIFIED BY NATIONAL SOCIALISTS as a significant threat was the Romani or, more accurately, the Roma and Sinti people. Known in German – derogatorily – as *Zigeuner*, or Gypsies, the regime could be sure that efforts to solve this 'problem' would be popular with many Germans. Sinti and Roma people experienced severe discrimination in many parts of Europe, as they continue to do today. Under both the Second Reich and the Weimar Republic there had been attempts to solve what was called the 'Gypsy nuisance' through legislation. In Bavaria, for example, Sinti and Roma were not permitted to move about without special permits issued by the police and were supposed to stay on designated sites; failure to do so resulted in the loss of welfare payments. Once the National Socialists were in power, the Sinti and Roma became the focus of growing research into what was increasingly perceived as a 'racial-hygienic' problem. Academics such as Robert Ritter of the University of Tübingen became the Reich's 'Gipsy experts'; Ritter would eventually head a research group within the Reich Health Ministry, and would be partly funded by the RSHA. The group's main task was to locate and classify Germany's Sinti and Roma population, without which state intervention would be impossible. According to Ritter, it was not just the nomadic lifestyle of the Sinti and Roma which gave them a tendency to criminality; this was part of their racial composition. He advised that they be re-settled in closed camps, as well as the sterilisation of Sinti and Roma people of mixed race. In a circular issued in 1938, *The Fight Against the Gypsy Nuisance*, Himmler confirmed that all Sinti and Roma, as well as other travelling people, were to be registered with the national police authorities, and that the Nuremberg laws applied to them, as well as to the Jews. The ultimate aim, he continued, was the separation of the Sinti and Roma from the German *Volk*. As in so many areas of racial policy, the outbreak of war saw an increasing radicalisation of policy: thereafter, Sinti and Roma people could live only on designated sites, and risked being sent to a concentration camp if they left them. There may have been discussions about killing them as early as September 1939, when Himmler chaired a conference on the issue. Certainly, Sinti and Roma living in Poland and Russia were targeted by the *Einsatzgruppen* when those countries were invaded. In December 1942, Himmler signed what became known as the *Auschwitz-Erlass* [Auschwitz Order] which ordered the deportation of all Sinti and Roma to a special subcamp at Birkenau. During the seventeen months it was in existence the camp was ravaged by epidemic disease, as well as becoming a focus of interest for the pseudo-scientific medical experiments of Josef Mengele. The camp was finally closed down in August 1944 when its remaining occupants, apart from a few kept back for work, were gassed.

Overall, the years 1933 – 39 did not create the racial utopia dreamed of by Germany's racial experts. There was simply not enough time to do so. Important as racial policy was, it was only one of the numerous areas demanding the attention of the National Socialist leadership. Even so, in these few years the task of separating racial and biological 'inferiors' from the mass of the German people had begun. Most important of all, the regime had succeeded in legitimising the fear and dislike with which many Germans regarded those who differed significantly from themselves. Long before the deportations and killings began, few were willing to protest, and fewer still were prepared actively to defy the regime. By this reckoning, 1933 - 1939 had been years of unparalleled achievement.

*In What Ways Was A Racial Community Created between 1933 and 1939?*

# Questions

- How far, and in what ways, did the National Socialist regime succeed in establishing a racial community in Germany between 1933 and 1939?
- Explain why different social and racial groups in Germany experienced different treatment between 1933 and 1939.
- "There is no evidence to suggest that Germany was any more or less racist than the average European country of the same period". How far do you agree with this claim?

# Chapter 5: Did Germany Conduct A Racial War Between 1939 and 1945?

## The General-Plan Ost

WELL BEFORE THE OUTBREAK of the war, planning began for the re-ordering of Europe under National Socialist rule. The plan was drawn up by the RSHA; there were several drafts, although the final version was not drawn up until 1940. No copy has survived, as most of Heydrich's RSHA files were destroyed at the end of the war. We know, however, that it consisted of two parts, the Lesser and Greater Plans. The first dealt with immediate issues, including the future of German-occupied Poland; the second dealt with longer-term policies to be put into effect over a twenty to thirty-year period.

Overall, the Plan involved the total reorganisation of continental Europe on a racial and biological basis. A vast area of Eastern Europe would ultimately be incorporated into Greater Germany. This would include much of Poland and the Czech lands, the Baltic states, and almost all the western Soviet Union as far East as the Crimea.

This meant that their native populations would be expelled, to be replaced by ethnic Germans. In 1942 Erich Wetzel, director of the Central Advisory Office on Questions of Racial Policy at the NS-DAP [*Leiter der Hauptstelle Beratungsstelle des Rassenpolitischen Amtes der NSDAP*] indicated that more than 50 million people would have to be moved. A few of them could be 'Germanised'; perhaps fifty percent of the Czechs, thirty percent of the Ukrainians and twenty-five percent of the population of Belarus. The remainder would have to be deported to western Siberia. However, the Plan was silent about many elements which were to be the defining characteristics of National Socialist rule. There was no mention of the Jews. Nor was there any mention of what was intended for the Romani, the handicapped or the huge number of prisoners of war which would inevitably result from military success in Eastern Europe. The Plan was not to be followed as if it were a blueprint for action; it declared a final goal and left the details to the future. As always in the Third Reich, policy was subject to improvisation, rapid evolution and constant interference from a host of mid-level and even minor decision-makers.

The rapid series of German victories that followed the invasion of Poland placed large numbers of Jews, Slavs and other 'undesirables' under German control. As the war continued, Germany itself began to fill with slave labourers from the East, who in National Socialist eyes would constitute a significant threat to the *Volksgemeinschaft*. From then on, these too became part of the racial question. The military victories of 1939-41 also enabled Germans to execute policy on a continental basis rather than, as hitherto, in purely German ones. From the point of view of Germany's leaders, it now made no sense to expel Jews – to take one example – from Germany alone; there would have to be a 'total' solution. The war placed vast areas, far from the German heartland, under the regime's control. Here many policies could be enacted without external interference. Within Germany itself the war created a perceived need, as well as opportunity, to expand vastly the euthanasia programme. Hundreds of thousands of those considered unworthy of life would be murdered.

The war itself radicalised many Germans. To give just one example, in July 1942 the men of German Order Police Battalion 101 surrounded the Polish village of Jósefów. Its commander then informed the battalion that its task was to kill all the Jews in the village – a 'frightfully unpleasant' task that he himself found highly regrettable. To stiffen his men's resolve, he reminded them that in Germany bombs were falling on women and children. Presumably the men were supposed to see an obvious connection between the bombardment of German cities by the Royal Air Force and the activities of the peaceful Jews of Jósefów. The assumption that they would do so turned out to be entirely justified. The battalion had not been involved in the killing of Jews before. It was largely composed of middle-aged men who had grown up long before Hitler had come to power. So they had not been exposed to the anti-Semitic propaganda that had deluged a younger generation of Germans. Despite this, and the fact that no one was forced to participate, only twelve men refused to kill. By the time the massacre was over, 1800 Jews were dead. There were many reasons why those Germans who did kill were willing to do so, but one reason was undoubtedly the feeling that the war itself seemed to legitimise behaviour that would otherwise have been unacceptable.

The war had from the beginning a strongly racial element: Hermann Göring actually described it as 'not the Second World War, but the Great Racial War'. He continued, 'The meaning of this war, and the reason we are fighting out there, is to decide whether the German and the Aryan will prevail, or if the Jew will rule the world.' There had still been some inhibitions left in the conduct of the war against the Western allies, but the war in the East was conducted with unprecedented savagery from the very beginning. In May 1941, during the planning of Case *Barbarossa*, the planned invasion of the Soviet Union, Herman Göring's Four-Year Plan Office circulated a memorandum that stated bluntly :

*Many tens of millions of people in the industrial zone will become re-
dundant and will either die or have to emigrate to Siberia. Any attempts
to save the population in these parts from death by starvation through the
import of surpluses from the Black Earth zone would be at the expense
of supplies to Europe. It would reduce Germany's staying-power during
the war and would undermine Germany and Europe's power to resist the
[British] blockade. This must be clearly and absolutely understood.*

The war would also involve the re-ordering of Europe's traditional ethnic and racial boundaries. Millions of ethnic Germans,
scattered from Transylvania to the Volga, would be returned to the
*Reich*. German colonists would settle the rich lands of Ukraine and
southern Russia. 'What India is for the British,' stated Hitler, 'Russia will be for us.' Thirty million Russians would simply have to
'disappear'; under the New Order, they could not be fed. The great
cities of Moscow and Leningrad [St Petersburg] would be emptied
and destroyed: there was no interest, Hitler said, in conserving these
large urban populations. The remainder of the Slav populations of
the East would be reduced to the status of hereditary slaves, and
moved elsewhere, if necessary, to allow the influx of Germans. It
was to be an early modern example of what has come to be called,
since the Yugoslav secession wars of the 1990s, 'ethnic cleansing'.

# Poland

JUST BEFORE *CASE WHITE* – the invasion of Poland – began, Hitler
summoned his generals and ordered them to close their hearts to
pity: 'Act brutally!' Just as would happen with the invasion of the
Soviet Union in 1941, the German army was accompanied by *Einsatzgruppen*. These were SS and police units tasked with isolating
and destroying perceived enemies of the New Order in Europe.
Hitler made his views on Poland clear in a meeting he had with Alfred Rosenberg, which the latter recorded on 27 September 1939:

*The Poles: a thin Germanic layer: underneath, frightful material. The
Jews, the most appalling people one can imagine. The towns thick with*

*dirt. He [Hitler] has learnt a lot in the past few weeks. Above all, if Poland had gone on ruling the old German parts for a few more decades, everything would have become lice-ridden and decayed. What was needed now was a determined and masterful hand to rule.*

The re-ordering of central and Eastern Europe on National Socialist lines began in Poland almost immediately. The *Einsatzgruppen* were specially equipped with small books printed on special paper with a tiny typeface. The books contained lists of all the Polish intelligentsia, including scholars, teachers, priests, communists, journalists and public officials, as well as prominent industrialists, bankers and even richer peasants. So were the members of the Polish nobility. Addresses and telephone numbers were included, as were those of close relatives. The SD card-indexes had never been exploited more effectively. In some cases physical descriptions and even photographs accompanied the names. These were the people who were marked for immediate arrest and, in most cases, execution. Within weeks, over 16,000 had been executed. The *Einsatzgruppen* did not work alone. Hitler informed General Wilhelm Keitel, head of **OKH,** that if the army did not wish to involve itself in these executions it must accept that the SS and the Gestapo would be working alongside. Despite occasional protests, the regular army co-operated in these measures and, in Poland, probably accounted for the majority of victims. On 2 October, Hitler stated that no Polish 'masters' would be permitted; where such people did exist, they would have to be killed, harsh though this might sound. 'Masters' included, in the city of Bydgoszcz, boy-scouts aged from twelve to sixteen, as well as a priest who attempted to administer the last rites to the victims. The purpose of such executions was partly to strike fear into the population, and partly to remove those elements least disposed to acquiesce in a German victory. By 1945, one Pole out of every five had died, a staggering statistic for a country that had been actually fighting for only three weeks. On 8 October 1939 Hitler signed a decree annexing large areas of western Poland to the Reich, including Danzig, West Prussia and the Warthegau. This was the signal for the first large-scale population transfers, as ethnic Germans were moved into the new provinces and Poles and Jews were moved out.

In 1941 Helmut Meinhold, of the Institute for German Development Work in the East, calculated that nearly 6 million Poles were surplus to requirements and were 'a waste of space'. He did not state – it was by now unnecessary – that they would have to be deported, killed or both.

## 'Life Unworthy of Life'

AMONGST THE TENS OF THOUSANDS of innocent Polish citizens murdered were those individuals considered to be 'life unworthy of life'. As we saw in the previous chapter, 'hereditary illness' was a widely-defined category. It included not just the mentally and physically handicapped, but those regarded as a social or biological threat to the racial community: the 'asocial'; the 'work-shy'; chronic alcoholics and those suffering from 'hereditary' diseases such as **schizophrenia**. Hitler had made it clear that he was only waiting for the outbreak of war to move against these groups, and here, at least, he was as good as his word. The so-called euthanasia programme can be divided into three phases: the killing of institutional patients in both Poland and Germany; the 'children's euthanasia', which was authorised even before the outbreak of war, and the systematic murder of those sent to purpose-designed killing-centres.

The killing of patients in psychiatric hospitals in occupied Poland accompanied the more general assault on the Polish population already described. It differed from the later euthanasia programme only in that no attempt was made to disguise these murders as medical events. An SS guard unit, or *Wachsturmbann*, was set up by Himmler in July 1930 under the command of Kurt Eimann. Its goal was to empty asylums and other institutions of their patients. In part this was to free up space for battle casualties, but Himmler also had in mind the need for temporary housing for the ethnic

Germans who would soon be moving into the occupied areas. By 1944 the Eimann group and others like it, had killed nearly 13,000 Polish psychiatric patients, mostly by shooting. The killing was not confined to Poland. In 1940 asylums in both Pomerania and East Prussia were also targeted. Unlike the Polish victims, however, these German patients were killed by gas in specially-adapted vans. The SS unit which carried out the massacres in East Prussia was led by Herbert Lange, who would later run the first death camp at Chelmno. The euthanasia programme was, in various ways, a rehearsal for the larger tasks to come.

# Child-Murder

THE MURDER OF HANDICAPPED CHILDREN within Germany was authorised even before the outbreak of war. In 1938, the parents of a severely handicapped child in Leipzig sent a petition to Hitler, asking him to allow the child to be put to death. The child was blind, lacked one leg and part of an arm and 'seemed to be an idiot'. The request was dealt with by the *Führer* Chancellery [KdF], run by Philipp Bouhler and Karl Brandt, Hitler's 'escort physician'. Brandt brought the matter to Hitler's attention – proof that such key decisions required the highest level of approval. Hitler instructed them to investigate the matter and to make a recommendation. They concluded that there was no justification for keeping such a child alive, and in due course the baby was given a lethal injection.

In August 1939 Bouhler and Brandt set up a committee for the registration of hereditary diseases, which rapidly introduced the compulsory notification of all newborn physically or mentally handicapped children. Once registered, reports on these children were to be forwarded to Berlin. It needed the agreement of three paediatricians to authorise a child's death. Such decisions were arrived at in an arbitrary fashion and often on the flimsiest of evidence. In October, Hitler signed a note which authorised Bouhler and Brandt to extend the powers of doctors to grant a 'mercy death'

– *Gnadentod* – to those suffering from illnesses deemed to be incurable. Significantly, the note was backdated to 1 September, the day of the German invasion of Poland.

More than 5,000 children died in this first phase of this operation. Ultimately, as many as 25,000 children were murdered. Death certificates were fiction: children were alleged to have died from measles or even, in at least one case, from warts. The victims were usually starved to death or killed by lethal injection, though occasionally children were simply left outdoors, where in winter they froze to death. In some cases this was done with parental consent; in others, the killing was not discussed with parents at all. It was not only the most severely handicapped children who were at risk. Children with cleft palates, stutters or other mild disabilities were often targeted. Doctors' research interests benefited from being able to carry out experiments on condemned children: spinal fluid and blood might be extracted and replaced with air, the better to show up on X-rays. Internal organs and brains were removed and sold to universities and laboratories. Julius Hallervorden, for example, chairman of the special pathology section of the Kaiser-Wilhelm-Institut, collected brains from 'mental defectives' and continued to study them until the late 1950s. The origin of this material was only formally acknowledged in the 1990s, when it was buried in a Munich cemetery. Hallervorden escaped prosecution and died in 1965.

There was much discussion about how open killing should be. The conclusion was that those suffering from serious mental and physical handicaps which 'aroused horror in others', should be killed without publicity. However, it was impossible to keep secret the murder of German children. A nurse at Kalmenhof-Idstein later stated:

*Everyone talked about it, even the children talked about it. They were all afraid to go to the hospital. They were fearful that they would not come back. It was a general rumour. The children played a coffin game. We were astonished that the children understood.*

The murder of Germany's handicapped children was the logical conclusion to a eugenicist programme which had begun long before 1933 but which perfectly appealed to Hitler and his supporters. There was nothing intrinsically National Socialist about the programme, which indeed for some is its most worrying aspect. Ideas of selective breeding, racial supremacy and the notion of 'life unworthy of life' had been commonplace since the mid-nineteenth century, and not only in Germany. The sterilisation of those considered socially or racially undesirable was routine, not merely in the Third Reich but in the United States until the 1950s; in Sweden until the 1970s and until still more recently in Switzerland. But nowhere else had this been extended to involve the murder of children. And it is unlikely that the medical profession in any other country would have taken to killing with the apparent ease of doctors in National Socialist Germany. Even Professor Gottfried Ewald, one of the few doctors prepared to publicise his objection to what was happening felt obliged, in a memorandum written in Göttingen in August 1940, to place his objections within a National Socialist context:

> *The role of the physician is built upon the urge to help another person, and not to harm him. Every sensible doctor will approve euthanasia. Who, however, will wish to be put in the position of eliminating hopeless cases against the wishes of their relatives and, without the most compelling need, taking upon himself the odium of killing? I can certainly kill any time if it is a matter of saving the* Volk. *I would also approve the elimination of serious criminals and common vermin.*

## Aktion T-4

THE MURDER OF INSTITUTIONAL PATIENTS, and the children's euthanasia, was followed almost inevitably by a full-scale assault on all others 'unworthy of life'. This was probably authorised by Hitler personally, though we do not have documentary evidence to prove it. These killings took place at carefully selected sites in

various parts of the country, such as Grafaneck, Hadamar, Bern-
burg, Hartheim and Sonnenstein. Experiments in killing patients
with carbon monoxide gas began in Brandenburg in January 1940.
Once these were successful, teams of T4 assessors visited psychiatric
institutions across the country. Although records were kept, they
were deliberately so inaccurate that it is now very difficult to say
how many handicapped people were put to death. Historian Susan
R Evans, who has made a recent study of those she describes as
'Hitler's forgotten victims', suggests that the figure lies somewhere
between 270,000 and 400,000.

As with the children's euthanasia, the murders - or at least the
details – were intended to be secret. The state judiciary was not
fully informed until April 1941, when Hitler's written order was
shown to them as authorisation. However, granted the numbers
of administrators, doctors, nurses, patients and relatives involved,
it was inevitable that T4 became public knowledge quite quickly.
Victor Klemperer, the Jewish professor from Dresden, recorded in
his diary in August 1941 that a friend's mother was showing signs of
dementia. The friend went on to say, 'I cannot put her in a hospital,
she'll be killed there'. Klemperer added that there was widespread
talk of the killing of the mentally ill.

A priest near Hadamar wrote of his concerns in 1941:

*Several times a week buses arrive in Hadamar with a considerable num-*
*ber of such victims. School children of the vicinity know this vehicle and*
*say: 'There comes the murder-box again.' After the arrival of the vehicle,*
*the citizens of Hadamar watch the smoke rise out of the chimney and are*
*tortured with the ever-present thought of the miserable victims, especially*
*when repulsive odours annoy them, depending on the direction of the*
*wind.*

It was significant that a priest wrote this, since many of the handicapped were originally cared for in religious institutions. Those
run by Catholics, who were forbidden to practice euthanasia in any
circumstances, were closed and their children transferred to killing
centres. Thus one of the few public expressions of dissent came

from the Catholic Church. Clemens von Galen, bishop of Münster, was an outspoken critic of the regime. In a series of sermons in 1941, he denounced it for its attacks on Catholic institutions and imposing a reign of terror on German citizens. On 3 August, he widened his criticism to include the deportation and murder of the handicapped:

> Here we are dealing with human beings, with our neighbours, brothers and sisters, the poor and invalids . . . unproductive – perhaps! But have they, therefore, lost the right to live? Have you or I the right to exist only because we are 'productive'? If the principle is established that unproductive human beings may be killed, then God help all those invalids who, in order to produce wealth, have given their all and sacrificed their strength of body. If all unproductive people may thus be violently eliminated, then woe betide our brave soldiers who return home, wounded, maimed or sick.

Three weeks later, Aktion T-4 was suspended. Hitler was not inclined to 'deal with' the churches at this stage in the war. Von Galen was left alone, though several priests who distributed copies of his sermon were executed. Although the gassing of German civilians was discontinued, local initiatives – the so-called 'wild euthanasia' – meant that the murder of handicapped adults and children continued until the end of the war. Indeed, the assault was widened. From April 1941, prisoners in the concentration camps who were considered no longer fit for work were gassed in the T4 centres, a programme known as 14f13. As many as 20,000 may have died as a result. The last known victim of child euthanasia, a four year-old boy, was murdered on 29 May 1945, weeks after the war had ended.

# Ghettos

THERE WERE ABOUT 2.5 MILLION JEWS in the General-Government; another half-million lived in the Warthegau. Ghettos in many of the major cities were established within a few months. The same policy was also followed in the occupied Soviet Union after June 1941. There were several reasons for the establishing of *Wohnbezirke* or 'living areas' for the Jews. One was simply to separate them from the rest of the occupied population: there was a widespread belief that resistance activity would always be led by Jews. Another was that Germans associated East European Jews with physical dirtiness, so that they were anxious to create a physical barrier between themselves and the ghetto inhabitants. Thus the creation of the ghetto was a security issue, but it was also one of physical and racial hygiene. Following a visit to Warsaw, Goebbels described the inhabitants as creeping through the streets like insects. 'It is repulsive and scarcely describable.' Reporting his impressions to Hitler the following day he wrote, 'The Jew is a waste product. More a clinical than a social problem.'

Historians disagree about the long-term purpose of the ghettos. Were they intended simply as 'antechambers to death', a necessary way to concentrate the Jews before their inevitable annihilation? Or were they intended – as the German administrations in the occupied territories sometimes claimed – to be fully functional, self-regulating mini-states for Jews? The answer, as so often with National Socialist policy, is that there *was* no strategy. Different authorities set up ghettos with differing and even conflicting purposes. For example, Friedrich Übelhör, governor of the Łódz district, wrote as early as December 1939 that the establishment of the ghetto there was only a transitional measure. He reserved for himself the right to determine when the city would be cleansed of Jews. The ultimate aim was 'to burn out completely this pestilent abscess'. Yet Łódz would become the longest-surviving ghetto in National Socialist Europe. Its highly productive population produced essential supplies for the German armed forces, so that the city's German mayor wrote to Übelhör in 1941 that the ghetto was no longer to be regarded as a holding or concentration camp, 'but as an essential component of the economy as a whole'.

The most controversial aspect of the ghettos remains the role played by the *Judenräte*, or Jewish Councils. In most cases, the Germans appointed small groups of Jews – sometimes, but not always, chosen by the community itself – to administer the ghettos. This included everything from overseeing the distribution of food to organising the care of the sick. Critically, however, the *Judenräte* also had responsibility for policing the communities, and for arranging the deportation of selected groups and individuals from the ghettos. Ghetto survivors, and subsequent historians, have often criticised those who ran these councils, seeing them as little more than collaborators.

There were many variations in exactly how the *Judenräte* interpreted these tasks. In some cases, the *Judenrat* was effectively controlled by a single 'messianic' individual, such as Adam Czerniakow in Warsaw; Jacob Gens in Vilna [Vilnius] and, above all, Chaim Mordecai Rumkowski in Łódz. Even here, there were wide variations in how such leaders perceived their role. Czerniakow committed suicide when deportations from the Warsaw ghetto began. Gens was a much darker figure. One inhabitant of the ghetto who knew him well stated:

*For quite some time we have regarded the Vilna ghetto as a barrel of gunpowder. Its inmates saw themselves as prisoners, not only of the German rulers, but of Gens as well. Gens added his yoke to the already harsh and strict regime imposed on the ghetto by the Germans. For all practical purposes he acted as the representative of the Germans. He introduced a regime of terror into the ghetto; this provoked the fierce resistance of numerous groups in the ghetto.*

Gens was executed by the Germans immediately before the liquidation of the Vilna ghetto in September 1943, allegedly for communicating with resistance groups inside the ghetto. Even Gens, however, was less controversial than Rumkowski of Łódz. Born in 1877, he was appointed *Judenältester* [Eldest of the Jews] by the Germans when, in 1940, they set up the Jewish ghetto there. Rumkowski rapidly seized control of the ghetto after it was sealed in May 1940, and began to run it according to his own ideas of what was necessary to keep the Germans content. His principal idea was to create 'a city of labour'. In his view, the Germans would not destroy a productive community. He quickly dealt with political opponents, particularly those who had belonged to communist or Zionist organisations. Such unstable elements were amongst the first to be placed on the lists for deportations from the ghetto which the Germans demanded. 'Dictatorship,' he asserted, 'is not an ugly word. With it, I earn the Germans' respect.'

Conditions within the ghetto were appalling, with a high death-rate [see the table on the next page] Nor did the population of the ghetto remain static. In addition to deportations, which sometimes removed as many as 20,000 people at once, there were new arrivals. In May 1942 large numbers of deportees arrived, having been expelled from Bohemia and the Warthegau; it proved extremely difficult to settle these in the overcrowded ghetto.

Rumkowski's administration had certain things to its credit: the ghetto was to prove the longest-lasting in the whole of German-occupied Europe, surviving until its final liquidation in July 1944. But for the delayed arrival of the Red Army, which deliberately halted its move into Poland, it is possible that the ghetto, which still had nearly 80,000 inhabitants, might have survived. Although rations were not shared equally – members of the ghetto administration, and especially the police, generally received more – the ghetto provided many thousands of meals daily. There were attempts to continue the education of children, and even to stage cultural events. Against these achievements, it is clear that Rumkowski's actions materially assisted the German administration. In September 1942 Rumkowski persuaded large numbers of parents to hand over their children for deportation. How much did he know about their ultimate fate? There was evidence available, and Rumkowski was in the best position of all to have access to it. Mass-murder by gas had begun in the nearby death camp at Chelmno in December 1941. Clothing from the victims of this camp was brought back to the ghetto for recycling; it must have occurred to those who worked on it to wonder what had had happened to its original owners. And it was Rumkowski himself who once remarked, 'If you knew what I know, you would not sleep at night. This way, I alone cannot sleep.'

| Month [1942] | Births | Deaths | Number of males |
|---|---|---|---|
| January | 34 | 1787 | 1083 |
| February | 45 | 1875 | 1124 |
| March | 54 | 2244 | 1411 |
| April | 31 | 4370 | 2050 |
| May | 58 | 1779 | 1068 |
| June | 99 | 1714 | 960 |
| July | 64 | 2025 | 1227 |
| August | 42 | 1738 | 1012 |
| September | 32 | 1074 | 608 |
| October | 21 | 860 | 474 |

TABLE 2: *Deaths in the Łódz Ghetto, 1942 [Figures from Gustavo Corni, Hitler's Ghettos, 2002]*

# Resistance

EXAMINING THE JEWISH councils of German-occupied Europe naturally raises the question of resistance. How true was it that, as Germans asserted, Jews went unresisting to their deaths? The commander of one killing-unit in Russia claimed that some of the victims would leap into the pits of their own volition. As we saw in Chapter 1, historians such as Raul Hilberg also considered that Jewish resistance was negligible. There was, however, more armed resistance than is generally imagined. Famously, in April 1943 the Warsaw ghetto resisted its liquidation and held out against an SS task force for several weeks, despite minimal armaments and little assistance from beyond the ghetto. As many as 13,000 Jews may have been killed during the uprising; SS losses were inevitably far fewer, but probably exceeded the 100 casualties admitted by commander Jürgen Stroop. Warsaw was not the only ghetto to resist: there was a brief uprising in the Bialystok ghetto in July. There were revolts in three of the death camps: Treblinka closed down after a prisoner revolt in August 1943, in which several guards were killed. In October, several hundred prisoners escaped from Sobibor after a carefully-organised plan succeeded in killing a number of the camp's key personnel. Sobibor, like Treblinka, did not resume its function once the revolt had taken place. And in August 1944, Jewish prisoners in Birkenau succeeded in partially destroying four of the crematoria before six hundred attempted to break out.

It should be much more surprising than it is that there was any resistance at all. Since the National Socialist regime itself was improvising Jewish policy until at least the summer of 1941, Jews could hardly be blamed for failing to anticipate the final outcome. The pressure to comply with German demands was huge. Perhaps the most important reason for this compliance was the lesson Jewish communities had learned from their own history. Jews across Europe had often experienced persecution and even massacre. Hard-won experience had taught them that the best possible response was accommodation. Persecution rarely lasted long. There was no tradition of armed resistance, and few Jews possessed weapons or knew how to use them. In any case, nothing in the history of East European Jewry could have prepared them for the ferocity of the German onslaught. The sheer extent of the unprecedented violence clearly had a kind of numbing effect, as indeed it was designed to do. Historians of the Holocaust often write about Jews as if they were somehow other than ordinary men, women and children. Jews reacted to the horrific scenes that unfolded just as most people would have done, with shock, disbelief and fear. But without weapons, violent resistance was not an option for most Jews, any more than it was for most of the people who found themselves under National Socialist rule. And the Jews of Eastern Europe were in the most difficult situation of all, since they were completely surrounded by actual or potential enemies. In many places local communities took advantage of the Germans' arrival to loot, expel or kill their Jewish neighbours and, quite frequently, all three. Jews who escaped from killing-sites or death camps had to assume that local populations were at least as hostile as the Germans, and sometimes more so. Some Jews were able to join partisans in Poland or the western Soviet Union, but there were plenty of such groups that targeted Jews as well as the Germans.

Resistance always brought reprisals. Following the Sobibor revolt, Himmler ordered the killing of Jews in the camps of Trawninki, Poniatowa and Majdanek. 43,000 were murdered in what was called Operation Harvest Festival; 17,000 of them at Majdanek in just one day. There was no such thing as resistance without victims.

Finally, it is worth pointing out that there was little in the way of German resistance either. In general, with some exceptions, Germans did not rise up against the regime because their handicapped children were being murdered, or because their neighbours were being persecuted for one reason or another. Resistance has always been a minority activity.

## Questions

- ❏ How far was Herman Göring correct in describing the Second World War as 'a racial war'?
- ❏ Why has the murder of the handicapped been described as 'the forgotten element of the Holocaust'?
- ❏ Why was there so little resistance to National Socialist racial policy?

# Chapter 6: Who Decided The Mass Murder Of Europe's Jews?

THIS HAS BEEN ONE OF THE MOST DIFFICULT QUESTIONS for historians of German racial policy to answer, even though it ought to be easy. After all, the National Socialist regime controlled a modern, highly bureaucratic state. In its twelve years in power, millions of documents were produced on every aspect of government policy. Such a key decision should have left a 'footprint' somewhere in the documentary record. And since it seems unlikely that such a decision could be made in National Socialist Germany without – at the very least – Hitler's knowledge and approval, a majority of historians has concluded that some sort of order was indeed given, and that this was done by Adolf Hitler. However, no document has yet been found which represents a clear and unambiguous order for the genocide. This is almost certainly because no such document ever existed.

There were a number of reasons for this. The most important was that the destruction of the Jews was always intended to be secret. References to it were habitually covered by euphemisms such as the 'final' or 'total solution'. The circle of decision-makers – at least at the highest level – was always small. Of course the genocide could not be kept entirely secret; nor was it thought desirable that it should be. As Hitler remarked on one occasion, 'It's good if the terror of extermination goes before us.' At a notorious speech given to senior SS officers in Posen in October 1943, Heinrich Himmler remarked, 'Most of *you* know what it means when fifty corpses are lying side by side, or a hundred, or a thousand.' So within the SS there were no secrets: the Jewish genocide, as Himmler remarked in the same speech, was a 'page of glory in our history'. But he also added that it was a page that had never been written and was never to be written. For the wider population, a degree of secrecy must be preserved. Much was agreed by word of mouth. Where orders and decisions had to be written, their circulation was restricted and – as with the minutes of the **Wannsee conference** – recipients might be ordered to destroy especially sensitive material. Even so, careful research has enabled some historians, at least, to reconstruct a likely sequence of events and decisions which resulted in the deliberate, systematic murder of several million Jews.

It is very important to remember that, for the National Socialist leadership, the 'Jewish question' was more than a *question*: it was a *problem*. The regime would not avoid or delay any solution for longer than it had to. Hitler himself commented in October 1941 that he had been forced to remain inactive against the Jews for some time: 'I'm forced to pile up an enormous amount of things myself. But that doesn't mean that what I take note of without reacting to it, simply disappears. It goes into an account; one day, the book is taken out.' This determination to act against the Jews was hard for outsiders – and even for some committed supporters of the regime - to understand. To them it made no sense that precious resources would be diverted, in wartime, in pursuit of this solution, or that by inaugurating mass killing the Germans would be losing an important supply of labour. But the war provided both the opportunity and cover for increasingly radical solutions: it was no argument for postponing them.

On balance, it seems unlikely that there was any long-term *plan* for the physical elimination of the Jews. But radical 'solutions' to the perceived problem of their existence emerged quite quickly. We have already remarked how, in January 1939, Hitler had referred to the possibility of a world war, and threatened that such a conflict would result in the 'annihilation of the Jewish race in Europe.' It is hard to be sure how literally such remarks were intended. But it is clear that the National Socialist regime intended, by whatever means, to remove the Jews – all the Jews – from its sphere of influence. The only question was how.

## Deportation?

THE EVIDENCE SUGGESTS that once the war broke out, plans for the deportation of all Europe's Jews were considered very seriously. Almost at once, planning began for the creation of a 'Jewish reservation' in the General-Government – the so-called **Nisko Plan**. An area in the Nisko-Lublin area of Poland was set aside to receive Jews, the first of whom were from Vienna and Bohemia-Moravia [in former Czechoslovakia].

In November, Goebbels recorded in his diary that Hitler had authorised the transfer of 150-160,000 Jews from East Prussia and Danzig-West Prussia to the General-Government, and noted that Hitler had laughed at this method of creating peace between their rival *Gauleiter*, who were now agreed on 'dumping their rubbish'. Nearly 47,000 Poles, both Jews and non-Jews, were deported over the next few months. In March 1941 it was the turn of the Jews of Vienna: 5,000 of them were deported to the General-Government. These, however, were to be the last for some time. For a variety of reasons, the idea of a Jewish reservation in Poland was becoming less attractive. The main objection was raised by the Governor, Hans Frank, who opposed any attempt to turn his fiefdom into a dumping-ground for what he termed 'riff-raff'. Frank urged, on the contrary, that the General-Government should be the first area made *Judenrein* – clear of Jews – and this was to be the principal demand of his representative, Bouhler, at the Wannsee conference held the following year. Once the invasion of the USSR had begun in June 1941, it made sense to Frank to suggest that 'his' Jews should be deported to the new territories that would be occupied, and this he did in a memorandum to Rosenberg in October 1941. Frank's view seemed to be supported by Hitler, who a few days before announced to his lunch guests that Jews from the occupied Czech lands must be sent further east than the General-Government and, like the Jews from Berlin and Vienna, would have to 'disappear'. Within weeks, beginning on 15 October, the first German Jews were being deported. Apart from the pressure created by several *Gauleiter*, who wanted Jewish property to re-house the victims of bombing raids, Hitler had another reason for deporting Germany's Jews at this time. He was anxious to prevent the entry of the United States into the war and the deportations from Germany, which were carried out in full public view, sent a clear message to the United States government – in his eyes a government controlled by Jews – that German Jews were effectively hostages for good behaviour.

The East was not the only destination considered for Europe's Jews. Another option, favoured until quite late in 1940, was the expulsion of the Jews to **Madagascar**, at that time part of the French colonial empire. This policy was first suggested by Department IV of the *Gestapo*, concerned with Jewish affairs and run by Adolf Eichmann, and plans were drawn up in collaboration with the Foreign Office. Not all historians agree that this plan was seriously intended, but the evidence suggests that it was and, moreover, that Hitler himself took an active interest in it. In June 1940 Hitler mentioned the plan in discussions he was holding with the Italian leader Mussolini. In July, Hans Frank, Governor-general of occupied Poland, evidently discussed the proposal with Hitler, whilst in August, Goebbels' diary recorded Hitler's wish to 'ship the Jews out to Madagascar', where they could set up their own state. In October, 7,000 Jews from the Saar-Palatinate and Baden were deported to France on Hitler's instructions; this may well have been intended as a first step towards their final expulsion to Madagascar. In the event, it was never tested. Although the conquest of France seemed to make the plan practicable, the continuing war with Great Britain, and the shortage of available shipping, soon rendered it unachievable. By December, when Madagascar seems finally to have been abandoned as a credible option, the overall situation in any case was pointing to still more radical solutions. Had it been implemented, the Madagascar Plan would clearly have been genocidal in practice. Millions of European Jews, with no experience of the tropics, or immunity to its diseases, could not have been deported to Madagascar without a huge number of fatalities. Nor was it likely that the native Malagasy people would have passively accepted the transformation of their country in such a way. Only a few years later, in 1947/48, there was a major indigenous uprising against French rule which cost a hundred thousand lives. Deported Jews would have been the first victims of Malagasy resentment.

The prolonged discussion about reservations, whether in Poland or in Madagascar, has been used by historians such as Christopher R Browning as evidence that there was no long-term plan to murder Europe's Jews. Even so, the proposals indicate that radical – and effectively lethal - solutions to the 'Jewish problem' had already surfaced within the German bureaucracy. If they were not adopted, this was for practical reasons and not because of any moral, legal or ideological concerns. There was only a narrow line between deportation and genocide. The establishment of any Jewish reservation in Poland would also have resulted in a very high death rate, just as the creation of closed ghettos was to do.

The outbreak of the war, as we have seen in the case of the 'hereditarily ill', resulted in the murder of those believed to be standing in the way of National Socialist ambitions to create a racially re-ordered Europe. Once it was clear that the deportation of the Jews was for one reason or another impracticable, it was almost inevitable that killing them would be the next step.

# Mass Murder in Russia 1941 – 42

FOR NATIONAL SOCIALISTS, the war against Russia that began on
22 June 1941 was to be, to use Hitler's expression, a *Vernichtungs-
krieg*: a war of annihilation. There were to be none of the inhibitions that had, to some extent, moderated the violence of the
campaign against the West the previous year. Rather it was the
brutal assault on Poland that would be the model for the Russian
campaign. On 18 December 1940 Hitler signed Directive 21, which
set out the objectives of Case *Barbarossa*. The directive was largely
about the strategic goals of the operation, and was curiously blood-
less in tone. Details of how the civilian population would fare, and
particularly the Jews, were left to a series of meetings in which
Hitler and his subordinates briefed the senior commanders in the
period before the invasion began. Granted what had happened in
Poland after September 1939, the invasion of Russia was bound to
be a catastrophe for the Soviet Union's 5 million Jews. Well before
the attack started, Jews were closely identified with the commissars
who, it was alleged, ran the communist state. It was also assumed
that Jews would lead any **partisan** forces that emerged to fight the
German forces inside the occupied territories. On 22 July, with
the campaign under way, Himmler noted in his diary that Jews
were to be 'exterminated as partisans'. In October, Field Marshal
von Reichenau also linked the struggle against the Jews with that
taking place against the partisans. Experience, he claimed, taught
that revolts behind the lines were always instigated by Jews. The regime was thus deadly serious when it talked constantly of the threat
posed by 'Judeo-Bolshevism'. In March 1941, Hitler's instructions
to Alfred Jodl, head of **OKH,** insisted that:

> *The forthcoming campaign is not just an armed struggle: it will also lead
> to the conflict of two world-views…The Jewish-Bolshevik intelligentsia,
> hitherto the oppressor of the people, must be eliminated.*

In consequence, Jodl issued guidelines to the armed forces which
made it clear that, just as in Poland, Himmler's forces would have
'special tasks' and would work alongside the army in carrying them

*National Socialist Racial Policy*

out. A few days later, at a further meeting, one participant noted Hitler's remarks as:

*It is a war of extermination. If we do not regard it as such, we may defeat the enemy, but in thirty years' time we will again be confronted by the Communist enemy. … Fight against Russia: destruction of the Bolshevik commissars and the Communist intelligentsia: Commissars and* **GPU** *people are criminals and must be treated as such.*

This was an invitation to mass murder. It is not clear precisely what instructions the leaders themselves received. Heydrich briefed them verbally before they set out for the front, following this up with written instructions issued in late June and early July. After the war, leaders of the *Einsatzgruppen* disagreed about precisely what instructions they had been given. By then, it would have been in their interest to insist that they had been following 'explicit' orders from Himmler to kill all Jews within the occupied areas of the Soviet Union, without regard to age or gender. Most, however, insisted that only Jewish men in party or state positions were to die, which accords better with what Heydrich had written. However, it must have been clear that any distinctions of age or gender would not mean much in practice. Jewish women, as well as men, were being slaughtered in central Russia as early as August, and even earlier in the south, where according to one local commander, 'suspicious females or Jews' were given 'appropriate treatment'.

Four *Einsatzgruppen* were established, numbered A, B C and D, and sub-divided into *Einsatzkommandos* or *Sonderkommandos*. They were officially under the jurisdiction of the RuSHA but controlled on a day-to-day basis by the RSHA. Himmler and Heydrich sometimes visited the front in person in order to supervise the process. On 30 June for example, both men arrived at Grodno in Lithuania. They expressed their displeasure that the local *Einsatzkommando* had so far killed 'only' 96 Jews. In July, according to **HSSPF** Erich von dem Bach-Zelewski, Himmler was in Bialystok, where he instructed local forces that all Jews, without exception, were to be liquidated as partisans. In mid-August, Himmler visited

Baranovichi, in modern Belarus, where he met again with von dem Bach-Zelewski, and left next day for Minsk, where he witnessed an 'execution of partisans and Jews'. On that day the leader of an SS cavalry brigade informed his units that Himmler had issued a specific order that all Jews were to be executed. The order evidently concluded, 'Drive the female Jews into the marshes': presumably a reference to the mass-murder of Jews now being conducted in the Pripyat marshes of Belarus. But even those commanders who had not received this 'explicit' order now realised what they were supposed to do. The 1st SS Brigade, for example, proceeded to kill 1,500 Jews, of whom 275 were women. On 15 August *Einsatzkommando* 3 in Lithuania also began to include Jewish children in the killing operations. Other units followed suit until, by September, the killing of unarmed children – who could not conceivably have been described as partisans - had become routine. By the end of the war at least 1.5 million Jewish children had been murdered.

The evidence suggests that it was unnecessary for Himmler to give precise orders to all his commanders. Instead, he delegated authority to the HSSPF and to the leaders of the *Einsatzgruppen* and other SS and police formations. He did so because he knew that they would respond as they did. This was unsurprising. The National Socialist regime had always encouraged relatively low-level initiatives and interventions, and policy was frequently improvised. Whatever initial restrictions were imposed, it was almost certain that before long all Soviet Jews would become targets.

The *Einsatzgruppen* worked alongside but independently of any *Wehrmacht* forces in the area. But the regular army, too, participated in genocidal actions, since it was by no means the politically neutral force suggested by its admirers. On the contrary, many of its commanders were convinced National Socialists. Field-Marshal Erich von Manstein, for example, informed his troops in November 1941 that 'the Jewish-Bolshevik system must be eradicated once and for all. The German soldier is therefore not only charged with destroying the power instrument of the system. He marches as the carrier of a racial ideology and as an avenger of all the atrocities which have been committed against him and the German people. The soldier must show complete understanding for the harsh atonement of Jewry, the spiritual carrier of the Bolshevik terror'. Wilhelm Keitel, head of **OKW**, demanded in September that the army should take ruthless and energetic measures against the Jews, 'the main bearers of Bolshevism'. Hitler was particularly impressed by Reichenau's order, referred to above. Reichenau considered that the most essential aim of the war was 'a complete destruction of the [Jewish-Bolshevik] means of power and the elimination of Asiatic influence from the European culture.' The order continued: 'the soldier must have full understanding for the necessity of a severe but just revenge on subhuman Jewry'.

Despite the assistance of the regular army, the great majority of the killing was carried out by the *Einsatzgruppen* and the other SS and police groups attached to them. There were differences in how large the groups were and how they were equipped: nor did all groups operate in precisely the same way. In general, however, the killing operations closely resembled one another. German units would arrive in towns or villages and demand the assembly of all Jews in the vicinity. Often – though by no means always – they would be assisted in this task by local nationalists eager to be rid of their Jewish neighbours, or to rob them of whatever valuables they possessed. The assembling of the Jewish population was often accompanied by extreme violence, intended to create terror and to lessen the likelihood of resistance. Execution sites were usually selected at a distance from the town: in the Ukrainian city of Berdichev, for example, a former airfield was used; at Ponary in Lithuania the Germans employed oil-storage pits some way from the centre of Vilnius. The area would be ringed with armed troops, police and, very often, local volunteers. Jews would be led to the killing sites on foot, or in trucks: one German recalled seeing an aged couple being brought in a horse-drawn coach. Where no pits existed, Jews were compelled to dig them themselves. Often the victims were ordered to strip. This was partly to de-humanise them and partly in order to make last-minute attempts at escape more difficult. Clothing would subsequently be distributed to local people. The murders were carried out by shooting. Machine-guns were used in some cases; individual rifles and pistols in others. Regardless of the exact method used, virtually all accounts agree that horrific scenes were unavoidable; that children were routinely bludgeoned to death to save the cost of bullets; and that many victims who had not been killed outright suffocated under the weight of the bodies that fell on top of them. Many people have subsequently asked how it was possible for 'ordinary' Germans to commit such atrocities. Research carried out by historians such as Christopher Browning and Omer Bartov suggests that most of the murderers adjusted to their task relatively quickly. Some feared to look weak in the eyes of their comrades; others feared for their promotion prospects. Drink played a crucial part. Some perpetrators – perhaps most – were brutalised by the process of war itself. In June 1941 General Lemelsen of XLVII Panzer Corps noted:

*I have observed that senseless shootings of both POWs and civilians have taken place. A Russian soldier who has been taken prisoner while wearing uniform, and after he had put up a brave fight, has the right to demand decent treatment.*

Only a few days later he was protesting that these summary shootings were still continuing, and were being conducted in 'an irresponsible, senseless and criminal manner'

Probably the important factor was that most of the perpetrators had been exposed for many years to National Socialist propaganda. In the East, they saw what they expected to see; primitive and dangerous 'sub-humans' who represented a threat to the Germany they believed they were fighting for. In letters home, many emphasised that they were doing to the Jews only what they fully expected the Jews would otherwise do to them. Lemelsen, despite having complained about the continuing murder of Russian prisoners, civilians and deserters, was still at pains to emphasise that his

**National Socialist Racial Policy**

soldiers' mission was to restore peace and order to a land which had suffered for many years from the oppression of a 'criminal and Jewish group'. People who had been identified as such should be shot – albeit only by order of an officer. Soldiers such as Lemelsen, and members of the *Einsatzgruppen*, might have been 'ordinary' Germans, but in the context of the East, 'ordinary' no longer had much meaning.

As *Barbarossa* proceeded, the numbers of Jews murdered reached extraordinary proportions. In October, more than 2,000 Jews were murdered by SS and police units in Mogilev. But that was only the beginning. By the end of the year, 190,000 Jews had been killed in Belarus. The same pattern was repeated in Ukraine, which was largely in German hands by the end of September. 23,600 Jews were killed in Kamanets-Podolsky in August, and more than 33,000 were killed at Babi Yar, outside Kiev, after the Ukrainian capital was taken in late September. The Jews of Berdichev were forced into a ghetto; this was 'cleared' in mid-September. Amongst the 16,000 people shot there was the mother of Vasily Grossman, arguably the greatest Russian writer of the century. Further south, it was the destruction of the Jewish community of Nikolayev which initiated the mass murder of the Jews of southern Ukraine and Russia. Visiting Nikolayev, Himmler assured the leaders of *Einsatzgruppe* D that the killing of the Jews was necessary to crush Bolshevism and to win territory in the East. In October, Odessa was captured by Germany's Romanian ally. More than 30,000 Jews were murdered in scenes so appalling that even members of the SS protested – not, of course, because innocent Jews were dying, but because the killing was proceeding in a chaotic and unregulated way. Much more could be achieved if the process of killing were made more systematic. On 1 December 1941 Karl Jäger, commander of *Einsatzkommando* 3, a unit of *Einsatzgruppe* A operating in Latvia and Lithuania, submitted a typical report. The report listed 136,421 Jews (46,403 men, 55,556 women and 34,464 children), 1,064 Communists, 653 mentally disabled persons, and 134 others as having been murdered between 2 July and 4 November. We know that such reports were forwarded to Hitler, and it seems highly unlikely that he did not know of their contents, at least in outline. This brings us inevitably to the question of Hitler's role in the unfolding genocide in Russia, and in the mass murder of Polish Jews that accompanied it from December 1941.

## *Führer* Decisions

THERE IS NO doubt that Hitler had helped create the climate in which murder on a very large scale was regarded as not only permissible, but inevitable. To give one example, on 16 July 1941 he attended a conference for those who would shortly be administering the Eastern territories. Hitler stated that the vast areas would have to be pacified as rapidly as possible, and this could best be achieved by shooting anyone who looked at Germans with the wrong expression on his face. Hitler's deputies also spoke increasingly threateningly about the likely fate of the Jews. In November 1941, in the journal *Das Reich*, Goebbels referred to Hitler's 1939 'prophecy' and claimed that Jewry was now suffering a fate that, though hard, was more than deserved. Compassion and regret were completely out of place. World Jewry, wrote Goebbels, was now undergoing a gradual process of extermination.

Creating the necessary climate for murder, however, was not the same thing as issuing orders to carry it out, although it might on occasion amount to the same thing. Historians want to know if Hitler actually ordered the killing of the Soviet Jews and, later in the year, the murder of the Jews of Poland and Germany. If they mean a signed instruction of the sort that had initiated the euthanasia programme in 1939, then the answer is no. No such order has been found and, almost certainly, no such order was ever issued. Verbal instructions, however, were another matter. Here there is compelling evidence that Hitler issued some form of verbal authority, though exactly when and how is a matter of dispute.

**National Socialist Racial Policy**

In general, historical opinion has been divided between those who favour such a decision as having been made early in the summer of 1941, and those who place it later that year. Support for the idea of an early decision came from Adolf Eichmann, who recorded in his memoirs that in July 1941 Heydrich had told him, 'I've come from the *Reichsführer-SS*. The *Führer* has given orders for the physical destruction of the Jews'. Rudoldf Höss, the commandant of Auschwitz-Birkenau, claimed that he was informed by Himmler that summer that Auschwitz was to become an extermination centre for Jews. On 31 July 1941, Göring signed a letter to Heydrich, authorising him to make all necessary preparations for the implementation of the 'overall solution of the Jewish question'. And claiming that the best way to understand the evolution of policy is to look at what was actually happening on the ground, some point to the escalating genocide in the USSR as evidence that Hitler had ordered the murder of Europe's Jews as early as July 1941.

However, these indications of an early *Führer* decision no longer seem quite as convincing as they did. It is clear that both Eichmann and Höss were mistaken in their recollection of the timing of the information they received. Höss's meeting with Himmler cannot have occurred as early as he stated, since he makes it clear elsewhere that the death camps in Poland were already functioning. Eichmann may well have learned of a Hitler decision, but he did not learn of it in the summer of 1941: the conversation with Himmler arose out of a visit to the Bełzec death camp, which was not yet functional. And Göring's letter to Heydrich emerged from a draft written as early as March 1941. It is possible – but not likely – that an expression such as 'an overall solution to the Jewish question' had the same genocidal meaning that it would have a year later. It is doubtful that words such as 'evacuation' and 'deportation' had yet acquired their status as euphemisms for deliberate and systematic mass-murder. It seems more probable that they referred to the possibility, still taken seriously at that time, that a 'solution' could be achieved by deporting Jews to Soviet territory once it had been captured. Nor is it clear that the mass-shootings in Russia were proof of an early decision for genocide. As indicated earlier in this chapter, the evolution of mass murder in the Soviet Union appears to have been chaotic and piecemeal. Certainly, within weeks Jews were being murdered regardless of their age, gender or political affiliation, and we know that *Einsatzgruppen* were increasingly under pressure from both Heydrich and Himmler to increase the overall number of Jews killed. However, it is much less clear that in the summer of 1941 a clear link had been made between the killing of Soviet Jews and the fate of those in western and central Europe.

There is a growing consensus that verbal instructions from Hitler were much more likely to have been issued later, in the autumn or winter of 1941. In this view, it was not the euphoria of victory that created the context for his decision, but the reverse. By the autumn of 1941 the global situation was changing. The war against the USSR was clearly going to take a good deal longer than had been imagined. The Russians were putting up more resistance than had been anticipated. In July, army chief of staff Franz Halder had declared the war virtually over; it was clear by the end of September that this was premature, and that whatever happened the fighting would not end before the end of the year. In the view of some historians, this was the background to a Hitler order – conveyed verbally to Himmler and also possibly to Heydrich – for the murder of all the Jews of Europe. According to historian Philippe Burrin, the order resulted from a murderous rage made more severe by the evident failure of the Russian campaign. Peter Longerich, on the other hand, links what he called Hitler's 'unwritten order' to the later events of December 1941. Hitler's war on Russia began to stall with the unexpected Soviet counter-offensive outside Moscow. At the same time, a world war developed with the German declaration of war on the United States. According to Longerich, this may have been the catalyst for Hitler who, according to Goebbels's diary for 12 December, was 'determined to make a clean sweep. The world war is here; the extermination of the Jews must be the necessary consequence'. Longerich sees this as further evidence for Hitler's direct involvement in the decision-making process.

It seems certain that policy changed after the summer, and perhaps that it was becoming clear that what was happening in Russia could also be extended to the Jews of Germany and the area under its control. In August, German Jews were forbidden to emigrate and, from September, compelled for the first time to wear the yellow star. This would make it much easier for them to be identified and, eventually rounded up. In October the first German Jews were transported to the East, despite the fact that only a month earlier, Hitler had refused to authorise it. One reason for this change in policy was that Hitler was under pressure from a number of quarters: some Party officials wanted Jews removed so that their apartments could be taken over by bombed-out families. More important, Hitler seems to have wanted the deportations to act as a warning to what he thought of as the 'world Jewish community' – which in his eyes included the government of the United States. The fate of Germany's Jews, he believed, might deter the United States from intervening in a war which was going less well than had been expected. German Jews were effectively hostages for the good behaviour of the United States.

Did the removal of German Jews signal that a definite decision had been made to kill them, as well as the wider Jewish population of Europe? Some of the 20,000 Jews from Germany and the Czech lands who arrived in the Łódz Ghetto were murdered immediately. In November and December, many more were deported to the Ostland, as the Baltic states and Belarus were now known. Again, large numbers were killed upon arrival in Kovno [Kaunas] Riga and Minsk. However, the evidence suggests that these killings were the initiative of local commanders in the East, who did not distinguish – as Himmler, for example, was to for at least a time – between Jews who had arrived from the Reich and the local *Ostjuden*. Conversations with Hitler recorded by several individuals at this time suggest that, rather than murder, he was determined that eventually all the Jews of occupied Europe would have to be deported to the East. Eventually they would be sent farther still, beyond the German sphere of influence in the occupied regions – presumably, to Siberia. On 24 September, Goebbels recorded in his diary that in the end the Jews 'should all be transported to the camps set up by the Bolsheviks. These camps have been constructed by Jews: what would be more apt now than to have them peopled by Jews?'

So when did plans for evacuating Jews to the East become a decision to kill them? The answer is probably in the autumn of 1941. It may have been related to the temporary improvement in Germany's war prospects: by late October, the advance on Moscow had resumed and huge numbers of Soviet prisoners were captured in encirclement battles at Vyazma and Bryansk. It was during October that a large-scale 'action' began which targeted the Jewish population of Polish Galicia; tens of thousands of Jews were killed in mass shootings which resembled those that were still taking place in occupied Russia. The Jews of Serbia were also targeted in October. Already for the most part in concentration camps, Male Jews were shot in increasingly large numbers as 'reprisals' for the killing of German personnel in Serbia. Thousands of Serbian Jews died in these mass shootings. In that month, too, it was decided to construct a camp with mass-killing facilities at Bełzec. Construction began in November, and in December T4 experts in gassing was transferred there. Initially, the Jews of the surrounding Lublin area were targeted: it was not yet clear that this would be extended to the whole of the General-Government. At the same time, a decision was made to empty the Warthegau of Jews: several hundred were killed in gas-vans at Kalisch, while the first Jews from the Łódz ghetto were murdered at Chelmno in January 1942. In December, the first Soviet prisoners were gassed to death at Auschwitz. Nor were German Jews spared. At the end of October, Himmler ordered that a transport of Jews from Berlin should not be liquidated: in part, presumably, because German Jews still had some value as hostages [See the

Documents section at the rear of this book]. His order came too late to prevent their immediate execution on arrival at Riga. It set a precedent. From then on German Jews, too, would be the victims as evacuation merged into murder.

October 1941, then, marked a number of significant and simultaneous developments in German policy. Mass shooting of Jews was extended from Russia to occupied Poland and Serbia. Camps built for the specific purpose of mass-murder were proposed and one – Chelmno – would be operational before the end of the year. Gassing ceased to be the brainchild of a single unit, but was becoming the preferred 'solution' for a number of senior officials. Experts in the homicidal use of gas were transferred to Poland. German Jews were in the process of deportation, and some of these were being murdered. All this was happening within the context of an intention to deport all the Jews under German rule to the East.

Historians agree that such decisions could only have been made or authorised by Adolf Hitler, who in turn was responding to the initiatives of his deputies and to the actions of his men in the field. The scale of the killing in the occupied territories may well have helped make it clear that genocide had become a practical possibility. In December 1942 Report no 51, was submitted to Hitler's headquarters. Ostensibly about the results of anti-partisan operations in Bialystok and Ukraine, the report listed 363,211 Jews killed in the period August to November. The report was re-typed on the special '*Führer*-typewriter' which had outsize letters so that Hitler would not have to use spectacles. The existence of this report does not prove that Hitler read it. It is powerful evidence, however, that his subordinates attempted to tell him what was happening; and this was certainly in line with an instruction issued in August 1941 by Heinrich Müller, the Gestapo chief, who ordered that Hitler be kept fully informed of the work of the *Einsatzgruppen*. Actually, there is no reason to doubt that Hitler both knew about what was happening and had authorised it. According to historian Mark Roseman, a shooting may even have been filmed for him. Following a *Führer* speech to assembled *Gauleiter* in December 1941, Goebbels asserted that Hitler had decided on a 'clean sweep' of the Jews. This, according to Goebbels, was 'no figure of speech. The world war is here; the inevitable consequence must be the destruction of the Jews.' In a later entry on 27 March 1942 Goebbels, stating that he was pleading for a more radical policy, claimed that he was, 'pushing at an open door with the *Führer*'. Ten days earlier he recorded that Hitler remained 'unrelenting' in his attitude to the Jewish question: the Jews must get out of Europe, if necessary by applying the most brutal means.

If it is hard to imagine that Hitler knew nothing about the mass shootings that accompanied *Barbarossa*, it is impossible to believe that he was ignorant of the 'industrialised' killing-process that was taking place from the end of 1941, as some 'revisionist' historians have claimed. The death camps required a significant diversion of resources, including transport, security and, of course, the 'expertise' of the perpetrators. We know that Himmler visited most of the camps; it is highly unlikely that he did not discuss what he saw there with Adolf Hitler. There is also independent evidence that Hitler was perfectly well aware of what was taking place. For example, notes made by Himmler of a meeting he had with Hitler on 22 September 1942 refer to the emigration of the Jews, and how to proceed further. The notes also refer to Odilo Globocnik, chief of the German police in Lublin: Globocnik was a key figure in setting up and overseeing the **Aktion Reinhard** camps in the General-Government; Himmler had ordered him to begin the construction of the first of these camps, Bełzec, nearly a year before. It seems improbable that when Hitler and Himmler met, and discussed Globocnik, they did not refer to what he had been doing over the preceding eleven months. It seems equally improbable that Hitler did not know what 'emigration' meant by that time.

Other evidence also suggests Hitler's knowledge of what was happening. On 12/13 April 1943 he met with the Romanian dictator Ion Antonescu. In a discussion of Jewish policy, Hitler insisted that it was necessary 'to proceed against the Jews, and the more radically the better'. Days later he was repeating much the same in a meeting with the Hungarian leader Miklós Horthy and Foreign Minister Ribbentrop. Arguing in favour of increased measures against Hungary's large Jewish population, Ribbentrop stated that 'the Jews must either be annihilated or taken to concentration camps'. Hitler joined in, pointing out that if the Jews in Poland were unable to work, they were shot. Jews must be treated like tuberculosis bacilli, which could infect a healthy body. Nor, in his view, was this cruel when one considered that even innocent wild animals such as hares and deer had to be killed.

Historian Saul Friedländer has written, 'The timing of Hitler's decisions was a matter of circumstances; the decisions themselves were not'. 1941 was clearly a year of decisions, however they were reached. The following year would see their implementation.

## Questions

- ❏ How seriously do you believe historians should treat the various proposals to deport the Jews of Europe?
- ❏ "Hitler, and Hitler alone, took the decision to murder the Jews of Europe". How far is this view supported by the evidence you have seen?
- ❏ Does the murder of the Soviet Jews prove that there was no such thing as an 'ordinary' German during the National Socialist period? Explain your answer.

# Chapter 7: Factories of Death 1942 – 45: What was a death-camp?

HISTORIANS CONTINUE TO ARGUE about to what extent the National Socialist genocide was unique, though there may not be much real purpose to this debate. Every historical event is unique in some ways, but most events also have parallels elsewhere. We know that several aspects of National Socialist racial policy were not unique to Germany. Many other countries based elements of their society on notions of racial superiority. Many people within those societies subscribed, sometimes unconsciously, to some idea of a racial hierarchy. Other societies discussed, and some even implemented, policies of compulsory sterilisation of those individuals seen as of lesser value. At one stage or another, many governments fretted over the financial cost of looking after individuals who for some reason could not or would not contribute productively to the community. And – both before and after the National Socialist period in Germany - several regimes showed themselves willing to use extreme violence against minority groups, sometimes with the intention of killing most or of all of them.

However, there certainly were unique elements to the National

Socialist genocide. Under no other regime did the issue of race dominate so much of everyday life. Far from being the peripheral element imagined by some of the first historians of the period, race was absolutely central. It underpinned policies in every part of the government's work from policing to paediatrics, and from war to weddings. Adolf Hitler regarded his 'discovery' that race was the central issue for humanity as his greatest gift to the world; and in his last communication with the outside world, the political testament he dictated in the Berlin *Führerbunker* just hours before his suicide, he urged the future leaders of the nation to adhere rigorously to the racial laws.

The death-camps were also unique. These have understandably become emblematic of the Holocaust. Nowhere else on the planet had such institutions existed. Never before had anyone even imagined that they could exist. It was not that camps in themselves were novel. In some ways the twentieth century was the century of camps. The British set up concentration camps for civilians during the Boer War. The First World War accelerated such developments. There were camps for prisoners of war, camps for refugees, camps for returning soldiers and camps for enemy aliens. From the very beginning of the Soviet Union there were so many camps that they formed a sort of separate world within the Soviet one – the '**Gulag** archipelago', to use Aleksandr Solzhenitsyn's memorable description. The Soviet camps – especially those in the far North, such as Kolyma - were appalling places. Prisoners were essentially worked to death. Only the very toughest, or the most fortunate, were likely to survive.

In the 1980s a dispute known as the *Historikerstreit* broke out amongst historians in Germany. Ernst Nolte, a leading historian of modern Germany, suggested that it had been the Gulag that had been the inspiration for the National Socialist death-camps. According to Nolte, 'Auschwitz was above all a reaction to the annihilating circumstances of the Russian revolution'. Others – notably the philosopher Jürgen Habermas - believe that this was no more than an attempt to minimise the Holocaust and to place the blame for it elsewhere. The National Socialist regime had no need to copy the Soviet example: it was fully able to act independently.

The first **concentration camp** was set up outside Munich, at Dachau, and it became the model for all the others. Run by Theodor Eicke of the SS, Dachau too functioned as part of a world within a world. Originally only political prisoners were sent there. Later, this was extended to cover all 'enemies of the state', including habitual criminals and those convicted of racial or sexual crimes. Once the war had begun, Polish and Soviet prisoners of war were also imprisoned, and prisoners were often hired out to nearby factories as slave labour. In 1933, the camp had a capacity of 5,000, but by 1942 this had swelled to 12,000. In the chaos of 1945, there may have been as many as 30,000 inmates. Although designated by the regime as a 'mild' camp, Dachau was notorious for its brutality. After Himmler took control of the camps in 1935, there was a change of regime, but – as historian Claudia Koonz points out – 'this did not mean an improvement in conditions, but it signalled the replacement of arbitrary violence with systematic cruelty.' Prisoners were beaten and brutalised, and subjected to physical punishment for the slightest breach of the regulations: forced labour in the nearby gravel-pits was tantamount to a death sentence. As in other camps, a gas chamber was installed in the 1940s, though there is no evidence that it was actually used. There is no question, though, that large numbers of prisoners in Dachau were killed: some were transported to the nearby mental hospital at Hartheim for gassing. Others died during experiments, carried out on behalf of the armed forces, to investigate the effects of high altitude or freezing on the human body.

Eventually hundreds – even thousands - of other camps were to follow Dachau and use it as their model. Recent research by the US Holocaust Memorial Museum suggests that there were many more camps than had been accepted until recently. There may have been as many as 30,000 slave labour camps and nearly a thousand concentration camps. Some of these, such as Mauthausen–Gusen, near Linz, or Neuengamme in Hamburg, effectively became death camps. Prisoners were worked to death in Mauthausen's quarries, mines and factories; they died on canal work in Neuengamme. The latter alone had almost eighty sub-camps attached to it, and Mauthausen had over fifty. So the recently-established figure of 42,000 camps of various kinds seems entirely plausible.

Only six camps, however, were constructed with the principal purpose of murdering Jews regardless of their capacity for labour. These camps did not all resemble one another, although there were certain common features. Chelmno was the first, to be followed by the *Aktion Reinhard* camps along the Bug river in Poland: Sobibor, Bełzec and Treblinka. All of these had closed by the autumn of 1943. The two other camps were Majdanek, near the Polish city of Lublin, and Auschwitz–Birkenau, both of which operated until they were overrun by the Red Army at the end of the war. These camps were unlike the other four, which had been constructed purely to kill as many Jews as possible and as quickly as possible. Majdanek and Auschwitz–Birkenau were also slave-labour centres and, at least initially, this was their main function. Gradually, in both places, the erection of killing facilities meant that the perpetration of mass-murder, especially at Auschwitz–Birkenau, became their principal purpose.

There were several reasons why the construction of camps for the specific purpose of gassing Jews was implemented. The most important was the experience of the massacres in Russia following *Barbarossa* in June 1941. Erich von dem Bach-Zelewski, HSSPF in the region controlled by Army Group Centre, expressed his concern to Himmler that his men were being brutalized by the killings and that they would not be fit for anything in future. There is some evidence that Himmler himself witnessed the murder of a group of Jewish women near Minsk in the summer of 1941. If his adjutant, Karl Wolff, is to be believed, Himmler was nauseated by the spectacle and by the fact that he was splashed with brain tissue.

If indeed this incident took place, it may have been in his mind when, at Posen in October 1943, he told an SS meeting that most Germans, unlike his audience, had no idea what it was like to see a hundred, or five hundred or a thousand corpses. It is clear that he was determined to find alternatives to the mass shootings which until the end of 1941 had been the principal means of murdering the Jews of eastern Europe.

Maintaining secrecy was another reason for the establishment of the camps. It had proved impossible to prevent evidence of the genocide leaking out in Poland and the USSR, just as it had been impossible to keep secret the euthanasia programme. Despite strict regulations to the contrary, German soldiers and administrators often photographed mass executions in Poland and the Soviet Union and even, on occasion, filmed them. In the Baltic states and Ukraine, local nationalists were frequently employed as executioners, and they were not subject to the same discipline as Germans. It was common for local people to witness the executions. So did German personnel who were not directly involved. The establishment of special camps would prevent such casual observation in the future.

Another strong reason to establish camps was that the technology for mass murder already existed. As Chapter 6 made clear, the T4 programme had employed gas to kill the handicapped at the 'medical' killing sites such as Grafeneck and Hademar. Gas-vans had also been used to clear the psychiatric institutions of East Prussia and Poland. The new experts in 'gassing technology' such as Franz Stangl and Rudolf Höss, could now be readily transferred to the bigger task in the East. Stangl ran Sobibor and was then transferred to Treblinka; Höss had command at two different periods in Auschwitz. Such people had already demonstrated that they had few moral qualms about killing for the state. Even if they had, they were now trapped by what they had already done. They too had become the bearers of secrets. They were not likely to refuse their new assignments, at which, it is worth recording, many of them excelled – and in fact there is no record of any of them having done so.

In 1941, *Gauleiter* Arthur Greiser had asked for a team of 'experts' to assist his desire to clear the Warthegau – especially the city of Łódz – of Jews. A task force led by Fritz Lange, who had been responsible for the clearing of psychiatric institutions in East Prussia and Poland, then brought the gas-vans to Chelmno, selected because of its proximity to Łódz and its relative remoteness. Chelmno, known to the Germans as Kulmhof, was the first functional death-camp, although properly speaking it was not a camp at all, but a stockaded group of improvised buildings centred on a manor-house. From December 1941, Jews were held in the manor-house and then loaded into gas-vans, where they were killed by exhaust fumes during the kilometre-long drive to a nearby forest. 300,000 Jews were killed by this method. There were only ten known survivors. In terms of sheer killing-power, then, Chelmno was the most efficient of the death-camps. Three gas-vans were used, each holding 100-150 people at a time. The bodies were first buried and, later, dug up and burnt. Racks were made of railway-track and the burning made self-sustaining by the combustion of human fat. This cremation process was so effective that all the later death-camps used it: the racks were used even at Birkenau when, during the killing of the Hungarian Jews in the summer of 1944, the mechanised cremation system broke down. Adolf Eichmann was one visitor to Chelmno. Twenty years later he recalled:

> *I followed the van and then came the most horrifying sight I've ever seen in my life. The van drew up alongside a long pit and the doors were opened and the bodies thrown out; the limbs were still supple, as if they were still alive. They were thrown into the pit. I saw a civilian pulling out teeth with a pair of pliers and then I took off. I rushed to my car and departed and said no more. I was through. I had had it.*

The camp remained operational until April 1943, when it was superseded by the establishment of the *Aktion Reinhard* camps. In the spring of 1944, killing briefly resumed there as the Łódz ghetto was finally liquidated: 10,000 Jews perished in this final spasm of activity, though by then most of the ghetto's inhabitants had already been sent to Auschwitz-Birkenau.

Adolf Eichmann may not have liked what he saw, but such scenes were considered a great improvement on those that had accompanied the mass shootings of the *Einsatzgruppen*. In details such as the removal of dental gold, the disposal of the corpses and the use of prison labour, Chelmno was the true pioneer in the search for a 'final solution'. The next killing-centre, at the industrial town of Bełzec, had already been selected as a permanent gassing-site some months earlier, probably as early as September or October 1941. It would develop the process still further. And preparations for the erection of gassing facilities in Riga were also put in train in October, a move initiated by the *Führer* Chancellery, the agency also responsible for the just-abandoned T-4 programme. Chelmno was a testing-ground for the programme of mass- murder that was now under way.

# The Wannsee Conference

ON 20 JANUARY 1942 a group of senior officials met in the Berlin suburb of Wannsee to discuss the implementation of an order signed by Hermann Göring the previous July. The order gave Reinhard Heydrich the responsibility of 'making all necessary preparations with regard to organisational, material and technical matters to achieve a complete solution of the Jewish question within the German sphere of influence in Europe'. Göring had not initiated this order: he had simply signed it, and Heydrich himself appears to have been its originator. It was as if the mass-murder of the Jews of the Soviet Union, now under way, had released the SS leadership from any lingering doubts about the course of the future. If it was possible to kill the Soviet Jews, why not those in the rest of Europe? Not all historians agree with this interpretation of the July order: in their view, it was simply an attempt by Heydrich to ensure that

SS control of Jewish policy would henceforth go beyond the frontiers of Germany. They point out that the order did not initiate any immediate change of policy: Heydrich did not even call a meeting until December 1941 and, owing to a change of date, it was deferred for another month.

This meeting is examined more closely in the Documents section. Historians are divided about its purpose and its significance. Those who attended it represented important elements of the party and state leadership, as well as the SS. According to Heydrich, who chaired the meeting, Europe was to be combed 'from west to east' in pursuit of Jews. Documents issued to participants listed Jews in every part of Europe, including areas not yet under German occupation. It was agreed that the _Führer_ had decided to end the policy of emigration: now Jews would be 'evacuated' to the East, where the majority would die from overwork and exhaustion. Those who survived would be 'dealt with appropriately': this clearly meant that they would be killed. There was also extended discussion of the future of the _Mischlinge_ – the half and quarter-Jews who had been living in uneasy limbo since the Nuremburg Laws of 1935. Adolf Eichmann, who wrote the formal minutes of the meeting, was quite clear that much of the discussion had talked quite openly about killing, so that it would not have been possible for anyone there to doubt what was in store for the Jews. Even so, this meeting was not – despite some early claims to the contrary – 'the meeting at which the Holocaust was decided'. As we saw in Chapter 6, most historians are agreed that this decision or decisions - had already been taken, and that it was Adolf Hitler who had done so. What French writer Patrick Desbois calls 'the Holocaust by bullets' had already killed well over a million Polish and Soviet Jews. Chelmno was already operational. So the Wannsee conference did not initiate the destruction process. Instead, it seems to have been an attempt by Heydrich to co-ordinate policy for the foreseeable future, and also to ensure that the destruction process remained an SS operation. In addition, their mere presence at this meeting turned these civil servants and party functionaries, too, into bearers of secrets. The SS would effectively control racial policy, but responsibility for its implementation was henceforth to be spread as widely as possible.

# Deportations

THE DOCUMENTS PROVIDED TO THE PARTICIPANTS in the Wannsee conference listed almost all the Jewish communities in Europe. It included Jews in areas not yet under German rule: it also included even tiny Jewish populations, such as the 200 estimated to live in Albania. The destruction of so many people – the final total was over 11 million - would involve an enormous logistical effort. Deportations to the East, of course, had already begun. Hitler had authorised the deportation of Jews from Germany and the Protectorate – former western Czechoslovakia – in September 1941, a decision that may have been precipitated by news of the expulsion to Siberia of the Volga Germans of the Soviet Union.

Adolf Eichmann was in charge of the RSHA's Department IVB4, which was concerned with all aspects of Jewish affairs, and he thus had operational control of the accelerating deportations from 1942. Eichmann's importance shoukld neither be minimised nor over-stated. He was indeed, as he himself claimed at his trial, a co-ordinator of the genocide, but he had little independence and was obliged to obtain consent for his plans from his superiors: Heydrich, and *Gestapo* chief Heinrich Müller. However, Eichmann was peculiarly relentless in his efforts to implement the decisions that had been reached. Department IVB4 was at the centre of operations as the 'Final Solution' moved unambiguously into mass murder. It managed relations with foreign governments; it liaised with the German transport authorities; it worked with the Reich's legal authorities to ensure that Jewish property left behind became the property of the state.

In January 1942, Eichmann referred to the ongoing evacuation of the Jews from Berlin, Vienna and Prague as 'the beginning of the Final Solution'. The first significant deportation of Jews from France took place in May. A month later, 'specialists' in Jewish affairs from France, the Netherlands and Belgium were summoned to Berlin, where Eichmann informed them that it was not currently possible to continue the deportation of German Jews to the East. In consequence, he ordered that Jews from western Europe – as well as from Romania – be deported to work as slave labour at Auschwitz. 15,000 Jews from the Netherlands; 10,000 from Belgium and 100,000 Jews from both the occupied and Vichy zones of France were deported. At the same time, the removal of Jews from Germany was accelerated. Large numbers were deported to the Theresienstadt ghetto, perceived as a transitional measure before their ultimate murder. Despite what Eichmann had told his specialists, German Jews continued to be sent directly to killing-sites in the East, where many of them were murdered immediately on arrival. The renewed deportation of Germany's Jews may have been the result of conversations held between Hitler and Himmler which took place at about this time.

In March 1942, Germany and Slovakia signed an agreement which allowed the deportation of Slovak Jews. These were held in improvised camps until they could be moved across the border into the General-Government. Approximately 58,000 Jews were sent from there to their deaths in Sobibor, Auschwitz-Birkenau and Majdanek. Deportations were halted in the summer, but renewed in October 1943, so that eventually more than 100,000 Slovak Jews perished. The summer of 1942 also saw the beginning of a process of deportation designed to empty the ghettos of the General-Government. At the same time, mass shootings were renewed in eastern Poland and the occupied Soviet territories.

The Jews of Romania had suffered from persecution since 1940, when border changes instigated by Germany had handed over some areas to the Soviet Union. Hundreds of Jews died in pogroms carried out in 'revenge'. Further persecution, including the dismissal of Jews from state employment, followed Romania's entry into the war in June 1941. At least 90,000 died when they were forced into camps in eastern Transnistria. But although Eichmann won the Romanian government's promise to turn these Jews over to the Germans, co-operation between Department IVB4 and Bucharest repeatedly broke down. By the beginning of 1953, it was clear that the war was turning against Germany: Romanian forces were amongst those which were destroyed at Stalingrad. There was increasingly little desire on the Romanians' part to proceed any further with the role Eichmann had assigned them in the 'Final Solution'. Thus, although 250,000 Romanian Jews were killed during the course of the war, few of them were actually deported to the death camps of the East. In sharp contrast the Jews of Salonika, in occupied Greece, were deported to Auschwitz–Birkenau between March and July of 1943, in such numbers that deportations from western Europe were temporarily suspended. In October came the turn of the Jews of Rome, an action rapidly extended to those areas of Italy under German control. Thrace in Greece, and Macedonia in Yugoslavia, which had been occupied by Germany's ally Bulgaria, were 'cleared' of Jews in March 1943: they were handed over to German officials, sent to Vienna and from there to Treblinka.

Frustrated in Romania, Eichmann pushed vigorously for the removal and murder of Hungary's 725,000 Jews. The Hungarian government of Admiral Miklós Horthy made a distinction between its 'own' Jews, and those who lived in recently-annexed areas, or had taken shelter on Hungarian soil. It attempted to deflect Eichmann's attention on to the latter, but it was not a distinction that interested him. His opportunity came when, in March 1944, Hitler ordered the occupation of Hungary in a bid to ensure its continued involvement in the war. Horthy, who remained in nominal charge in Hungary despite the occupation, agreed to deliver 100,000 Hungarian Jews for use as slave labour; and Eichmann himself arrived in Budapest a few days later. Discussions on how to implement the deportation of Hungary's Jews began in April. It had been clear from the beginning that the occupying forces were after a great deal more than simply slave labourers. They wished to remove the Jews from Hungary altogether. This was certainly the view of Ernst Kaltenbrunner, Heydrich's successor as head of the RSHA. In his view, the mere existence of such a large, intact Jewish population was a threat to the war effort, and itself explained the reluctance of the Hungarians to prosecute the war more vigorously.

Hungary was divided into six zones. In each, Jews were rounded up between April and July, and transferred to makeshift camps and improvised ghettos. The first deportations began on 15 May, and the plan was that 3,000 Hungarians Jews would arrive at Auschwitz-Birkenau every day. In his post-war memoir, Eichmann recalled that, 'Despite all the interventions, the deportation rolled with regularity. So I fulfilled the order of the *Reichsführer-SS*: nothing else mattered'. A special railway spur was built at Birkenau so that trains from Hungary could arrive right inside the camp, and within walking distance of the gas-chambers. Between may and July, over 437,000 Hungarians Jews were murdered there. By then, the only Jews remaining in Hungary were those in Budapest, and those who were working as forced labour for the Germans. Of these, many died when the Germans replaced Horthy with Ferenc Szálasi in October. Szálasi and his fascist Arrow Cross movement murdered many of the surviving Jews in the few months they were in power.

In January 1942, at the Wannsee conference, Reinhard Heydrich had stated that Europe would be combed through from west to east in the practical execution of the 'Final Solution'. Despite the many practical and political obstacles in their way, his listeners had for the most part succeeded in doing precisely that.

## The *Aktion Reinhard* camps

THREE MORE CAMPS, all with permanent gassing facilities, were established during 1942. These were at Bełzec, Sobibor and Treblinka, all located near the river Bug and – though in rural locations

– relatively close to large population centres. Their main function was the destruction of the Jews of Poland, though in time Jews from western Europe – especially the Netherlands – were also murdered in Treblinka. The *Aktion Reinhard* camps rapidly developed a system so efficient that at least one survivor believed that, if necessary, the Treblinka camp alone could have killed all the Jews that the regime planned to kill. It is worth remembering that at the beginning of 1942, most of the Jews who were to die in the Holocaust were still alive. By the end of that year, the situation was entirely changed: the majority of all Jewish deaths in the Holocaust had already taken place.

Most of those who died in the death-camps were transported by rail: indeed the killing-sites were usually located near major rail-junctions. The highly efficient railway directorate charged the standard third-class fare for each Jew transported; one-way for the Jews but the return fare for their guards. Children under the age of ten went at half-fare and children under four went free. The standard adult fare was 4 *pfennig* for adults, though trains carrying 400 'passengers' or more received a 50% discount. In the process the railways made a good deal of money. Transport secretary and *Reichsbahn* deputy director Albert Ganzemüller was the only railway official to face post-war prosecution for his role in the Holocaust. He suffered a heart attack on his first day in court, was judged unfit to plead, and was left in peace for his remaining twenty-three years of life. The trains themselves were more than simply a means of conveyance. They were grossly over-crowded; stiflingly hot in summer but unheated in winter. The notorious cattle-wagons were sealed from the outside and did not possess even basic sanitation. Food and water were not supplied. One worker in Treblinka described how these trains arrived at the camp surrounded by a sort of va-pour-cloud arising from the tightly-packed prisoners. It was inevitable that a significant proportion of them, especially the very old, the very young and the sick, died on board. The trains themselves had become an instrument of genocide: a remarkable achievement for a technology only a century old.

Each camp developed procedures for 'handling' the transports as they came in. At all of them some sort of selection process was undertaken to determine which of the prisoners could be usefully employed for the work that the regular personnel were unwilling or unable to perform themselves, including the disposal of corpses and the maintenance of the camp buildings. Most prisoners, however, were destined for immediate destruction. In what became well-versed routines, prisoners de-trained and were progressively deprived of their possessions, including their luggage, their clothing and even their hair, which was used to make felt slippers for the crews of U-boats. The loss of their clothes and their segregation by age and sex caused immediate disorientation. So did the mixture of seeming normalcy – at Treblinka, there was even a fake railway station, complete with flower-beds – and sudden, apparently random violence. Prisoners were assured that they would come to no harm and would be put to work. This was often followed by instructions to shower. Where necessary, whips were used to 'herd' the prisoners and to secure compliance. The existence of the gas-chambers was hidden until the last possible moment: they were usually separated in some way from the rest of the camp. In Sobibor the area was known as the *Totenlager*. It could only be approached by means of a path that snaked through tall barbed-wire fences that were interwoven with tree-branches. A similar arrangement existed at Treblinka, where the path was known as the 'Tube' or as the 'Way to Heaven'. Once victims were in the 'Tube', they were doomed.

Bełzec opened on 17 March 1942. It used six gas chambers which pumped carbon monoxide gas over their victims. 15,000 people a day could be 'processed', although the frequent failure of the engines supplying the gas meant that in May and June 1942 Bełzec was not able to operate at all. It was closed down in November 1942, being replaced by the more efficient Auschwitz-Birkenau. In 1997/98 Bełzec was partially excavated by trained archaeologists.

*National Socialist Racial Policy*

They found mass graves containing cremated human remains, as well as largely-intact bodies which still retained flesh and hair: the excavations confirmed the few eyewitness accounts of the camp and its operation. It also confirmed that killing in the death-camps was not quite the 'industrialised' model of popular imagination, which was always an excessively sanitised version of the truth. The greasy pits of human fat and body-wax were the product of a system which frequently broke down. Even so, this 'primitive' camp, sixty miles from Warsaw, was able to kill 600,000 people in the short period it was operational.

Sobibor, seventy kilometres south-east of Warsaw, was operational from 8 May 1942 and was closed down at the end of 1943. During that time it killed more than a quarter of a million people. It would undoubtedly have killed more but for the revolt that effectively terminated its existence on 14 October 1943. The revolt was not wholly without parallel: a special commando in Birkenau also revolted in October 1944. But the Sobibor rebels killed several guards and SS personnel and enabled several hundred prisoners to escape. The camp closed just four days later. It was a remarkable feat of cold-blooded courage and resourcefulness.

Treblinka, the last of the *Aktion Reinhard* camps, represented 'the victory of the technicians', according to historian Konnilyn G Feig. The camp, 120 kilometres northeast of Warsaw, began operation in July 1942 and, by the time it closed eighteen months later, may have killed as many as 870,000 Jews. It was commanded by Franz Stangl, who had previously run Sobibor, and was used to kill the Jews removed from the Warsaw ghetto. Stangl used his previous experience as an organiser of *Aktion T-4* and at Sobibor to ensure that Treblinka was operated with maximum efficiency. Everything was done to avoid panicking the prisoners. Initially, there were three gas-chambers, which killed their victims using carbon-monoxide gas pumped from the engines of captured Russian tanks. Ultimately there would be six, capable of killing 6,000 prisoners at a time. Perhaps 870,000 were murdered there. Like Sobibor, the camp was

closed following a revolt of camp workers in August 1943. Several
hundred succeeded in escaping, although only twenty would survive the war. By then Treblinka's work was done. One of its guards
kept a photograph album of the camp. He titled it fondly: 'Those
Were The Days'.

## Auschwitz-Birkenau: Destructive Dynamism

AUSCHWITZ, IN UPPER Silesia, has become the emblematic camp
of the Holocaust, and with reason. In fact there were three main
camps, as well as 28 local subsidiaries. Auschwitz 1, a former Polish
army barracks, was mainly used to hold first Polish prisoners, and
later, Soviet prisoners of war. It was also, bizarrely, a place selected by Himmler as the site for agricultural experiments, despite its
proneness to flooding. In November 1940 the industrial combine
I G Farben also declared its interest in the area as a site for the
production of synthetic rubber: this would lead to the creation of
Auschwitz III, at nearby Monowitz. Orders for the construction of
Auschwitz II, at Birkenau, were issued in September 1941. At first,
Birkenau was also designed simply to hold Soviet prisoners; there
was no indication that it would become a killing-ground for Jews.

However, experimental killing of prisoners by cyanide gas had
already begun in Auschwitz 1. Zyklon B was a highly efficient pes-
ticide, already in use in Germany's camps for delousing clothing.
'Unproductive' Jews from the locality were also murdered, beginning in the autumn of 1941. Early the following year, the first
killing-facilities were built at Birkenau; two small cottages rough-
ly converted into gas-chambers. These were used to murder Jews
sent from Slovakia, as well as several transports of Jewish children
from France in August 1942. Throughout 1942, Auschwitz was a
less significant killing-centre than the *Aktion Reinhard* camps. But
by the spring of 1943, this began to change. Increasingly, there was
a demand for Jewish labour, as well as for their eventual murder.
The Auschwitz complex was well-suited to these twin goals. Jews

could be selected for work or death on arrival. Those chosen for work could be sent to Monowitz or any of the growing number of nearby sub-camps. Once they were no longer productive, they could be sent to Birkenau. In March 1943, the first purpose-built killing-facility was opened there. Originally designed as a mortuary, its basement was altered to function as an underground undressing-room and gas-chamber. At ground level there was a crematorium with five ovens, each with three furnace doors. This was *Krema* 2; it was soon joined by *Krema* 3. Two more crematoria were constructed near the two improvised cottages: here the killing facilities were at ground level. In all, the four new Birkenau crematoria could 'process' 4,700 people a day, or nearly 150,000 a month. In fact Birkenau was never as efficient as this suggests. *Kremas* 4 and 5 broke down repeatedly, and corpses had to be disposed of by burning, as at Treblinka.

By the summer of 1944, about 500,000 people – 90% of them Jews – had been murdered at Birkenau. But it was the murder of the Hungarian Jews in the spring and summer of 1944 that would make it the greatest mass-murder site in history. Hungary was always regarded as an unreliable ally by the Germans, and had been particularly unwilling to act against the 760,000 Jews who lived there. German forces occupied the country in March 1944, responding to fears that the Hungarian leadership was considering making peace. Hungary's raw materials were also a major consideration. A high-powered RSHA team in Budapest, led by Adolf Eichmann, demanded the deportation of Hungary's 760,000 Jews, which began at the end of May 1944. By the end of the summer, more than 437,000 had been deported to Birkenau; the great majority of them were gassed within hours of arrival.

This 'frenzied killing' was a last spasm. Selection and gassing ceased in November 1944. The last transport arrived in January 1945. With the Red Army approaching, the crematoria were destroyed a few days later and the bulk of the survivors were moved out.

*Factories of Death 1942 – 45: What was a death-camp?*

# End: 'Liberation'

FOR THE MOST PART the death-camps were liberated in the closing months of the war. 'Liberated' is a term of variable usefulness in this context. The *Aktion Reinhard* camps were empty and had, indeed, already ceased to exist. At Treblinka the gas chambers – the only permanent buildings in the camp – had been torn down in 1943 and a small forest planted. A farmhouse was built and an elderly couple shipped in to occupy it: they were supposed to state, if they were ever questioned, that they had always lived there. It proved impossible, however, to conceal the piles of ash and half-cremated bone. Nor could local people be prevented from digging holes all over the site in search of gold; a few years after the war and the former camp looked like anything but an old farmstead.

Soviet forces entered Majdanek on 22 July1944. It was the first capture of a camp still containing all the machinery of mass-murder. For the first time the outside world saw gas chambers disguised as showers, and huts filled with clothing and other possessions. The crematoria still contained human residue. So when Auschwitz-Birkenau was reached, on 27 January 1945, it did not create the same sense of shock. Most of the surviving inmates had been moved as the Red Army approached. Even so, there were still several thousand prisoners existing in conditions of unimaginable squalor. A few months later it was the turn of the British and Americans to encounter camps at Bergen-Belsen, Buchenwald and, on 29 April 1945, Dachau itself. Although these were not death-camps, they contained many people who had been evacuated from them. These evacuations have been more properly termed **'death marches'**. Hundreds of thousands of prisoners were marched through the worst of the winter from one camp to another, often with no discernible final destination. In reality, of course, the aim was to kill as many of them as possible. Along the way those who could not keep up were subject to summary execution. Many Germans must have seen these appalling processions in the final months and weeks of the war: it made later protestations that no one in Germany had known the fate of the prisoners difficult to believe. The discovery of these camps, ravaged by disease, filled with skeletal prisoners and rotting corpses, created some of the defining images of the fate of Europe's Jews. The films and photographs were to some extent misleading. They suggested that all the camps were similar, and that they had all been established for the same purpose. This was not the case. These were camps overwhelmed, in the last weeks of the war, by vast numbers of prisoners from widely varying locations and backgrounds. No one, not the guards and certainly not the liberators, could tell which of the thousands of bodies were Jewish and which were not. They certainly included, in addition to Jews, people from virtually all the categories that Germans had been taught to regard as racially and socially undesirable. But they obscured the central role that Jews had had in the National Socialist world-view.

## What Did the Allies Know?

THIS IS A CONTROVERSIAL QUESTION, though in fact the answer to it is relatively straightforward. The Allied governments had a very good idea about what was happening in the East, and they did so quite early. Thanks to the decrypting of the German military codes, they were able to intercept Order Police signals as early as September 1941which made it clear that Jews in the Soviet Union were being systematically murdered. In order not to reveal that the codes had been broken, no further action was taken. Over the next year, however, Polish underground sources brought further information to London and Washington, including detailed eyewitness description of death-camps such as Treblinka and Birkenau.

However, when historians ask what the Allies knew, they are usually asking another question as well, which is, 'And why did they do nothing?' There were a number of reasons for Allied inactivity. Anti-Semitism undoubtedly existed at various levels in all the Allied governments. The British Foreign Secretary, Anthony Eden, was more anxious about the possibility of Britain's being asked to accept thousands more Jews than he was about the likelihood of their murder. 'I am sorry to bother you about Jews…I know what a bore this is', one of his junior ministers wrote to him. This sort of reflex anti-Semitism was widely shared by officials in both Britain and the United States. However, it was not the sole, or even the main, reason for Allied inactivity. One factor, particularly affecting the Western allies, was the fact that they had limited experience of large-scale atrocities in their own recent history. For British decision-makers, the most obvious comparison ought to have been with the German atrocities of the First World War. Though they were on a vastly smaller scale, German actions in Belgium and France at that time would actually have been a good starting-point for examining what was happening in the 1940s. In 1914, German military authorities had shown complete contempt for international law, and a willingness to resort very rapidly to extreme violence. Its readiness to target civilian populations would have been recognisable to anyone looking at what was taking place in Poland and Russia after 1939. But almost everyone believed that the reports of 1914 had been exaggerated, and officials were keen to avoid acting on the basis of what they feared might yet turn out to be similarly inflated reports. Without such a comparison, what was happening was literally inconceivable to middle-class Britons and Americans. It was beyond anything imagined even by the Soviets, who had their own camps and a very recent – indeed, continuing – history of massive, state-sanctioned violence. The result was that the Allies tended to speak firmly but find reasons not to do very much. In London, Eden made a statement to Parliament in December 1942, in which he outlined the deportations and mass-murder of Europe's Jews. MPs were invited to stand as a mark of respect for the victims. It was an impressive moment, but it was not translated into the direct action that some demanded, such as bombing the camps or at least the rail lines leading to them. It was equally true that precision bombing was in its infancy during the Second World War, and often resulted in heavy casualties for little obvious gain.

**National Socialist Racial Policy**

And there was something to be said for the view that the defeat of Germany was likely to be the quickest way to end the genocide. Even so, it is hard to resist the conclusion that more might have been done even before the end of the war.

## Questions

- How convincing do you find the argument of historians such as Martin Gilbert that more could have been done by the allies to disrupt the operation of the death-camps?
- How convincing do you find the view that the construction of the death-camps was what made the Holocaust unique?
- 'Future generations may see Auschwitz as just another bad thing that happened in the past. But that should not be allowed to happen.' How far do you agree with this view?

# Looking At Documents:

## 1. The Wannsee Protocol [Shortened]

Stamp: Top Secret
30 Copies
16<sup>th</sup> Copy
Minutes of Discussion

The following persons took part in the discussion about the final solution of the Jewish question which took place in Berlin, Am Großen Wannsee No. 56/58 on 20 January 1942.

*Gauleiter* Dr Meyer and *Reichsamtleiter* Dr Leibbrandt, Reich Ministry for the Occupied Eastern Territories
State Secretary Dr Stuckart, Reich Ministry for the Interior
State Secretary Neumann, Plenipotentiary for the Four-Year Plan
State Secretary Dr Bühler, Office of the General-Government
Under-State Secretary Dr Luther, Foreign Office
*SS-Oberführer* Klopfer, Party Chancellery
Ministerial Director Kritzinger, Reich Chancellery
*SS-Gruppenführer* Hofmann, RuSHA
*SS-Gruppenführer* Müller
*SS-Obersturmbannführer* Eichmann, RSHA
 *SS-Oberführer* Dr Schöngarth, Chief of the *Sipo* and SD in the General-Government
*SS-Sturmbannführer* Dr Lange, Commander of the Sipo and SD for Latvia

At the beginning of the discussion Chief of the Security Police and of the SD, *SS-Obergruppenführer* Heydrich, reported that the Reich Marshal [Göring] had delegated to him the preparations for the Final Solution of the Jewish question in Europe and that this discussion had been called for the purpose of clarifying fundamental questions.

Overall control of the Final Solution of the Jewish Question, regardless of geographical boundaries, with the *Reichsführer-SS* and Chief of the German Police [Himmler].

The Chief of the Security Police and of the SD then gave a short report of the struggle which thus far had been carried on against this enemy, the essential points being:

The expulsion of the Jews from every sphere of life of the German *Volk*.

The expulsion of the Jews from the living-space of the German *Volk*.

Instead of emigration, the new solution has emerged, after prior approval by the *Führer*, of evacuating Jews to the East.

These actions are nevertheless to be seen only as temporary relief, but they are providing the practical experience which is of great importance for the coming Final Solution of the Jewish question.

Approximately eleven million Jews will be involved in the Final Solution of the European Jewish question…

In the course of the Final Solution and under appropriate leadership, the Jews should be put to work in the East. In large, single-sex labour columns, Jews fit to work will work their way eastwards constructing roads. Doubtless the large majority will be eliminated by natural causes. Any final remnant that survives will doubtless consist of the most resistant elements. They will have to be dealt with appropriately because otherwise, by natural selection, they would form the germ cell of a new Jewish revival. (See the experience of history.)

## Commentary

IN 1947 AMERICAN LEGAL EXPERTS were still combing the German archives for evidence to be used in the continuing Nuremberg trials. When this document was discovered, one of them memorably described it as 'perhaps the most shameful document of modern history'. A small group of high-ranking officials of the National Socialist regime had met five years earlier to discuss the murder of Europe's eleven million Jews. Since then, the Wannsee conference has become infamous. At least two films have been made of it, and it has been the subject of a number of specialist studies, as well as a best-selling thriller.

The Protocol, it need hardly be said, was never intended to be read outside a very small number of people. Only one copy survived the war: that of Martin Luther [no relation of the Protestant reformer], which was discovered in the records of the Foreign Office. It has sometimes been described as the 'smoking gun' of Holocaust studies. For many years it was presented as the moment when the mass-murder of Europe's Jews was decided. However, it is a rather more puzzling document than this suggests.

Students need to be aware, first of all, that even the full document is only a summary of the discussion. The meeting lasted less then two hours and was interrupted by alcoholic refreshments. Eichmann wrote the summary, known to historians as the Protocol. It was then amended by Heydrich. Such a record contains only the barest outline of what was said. It cannot reproduce important elements of the meeting. We do not know precisely what each participant said, nor what tone of voice was used when saying it. There were probably small-scale discussions between individuals, but these are not recorded either. On trial in Jerusalem, nearly twenty years later, Eichmann agreed that methods of killing had been discussed; that some of the language used had been 'over-plain' and that he had changed this in the Protocol so that it was more like 'office-language'. At least half the document – not reproduced here – is taken up with an extended discussion of what was to happen to the half- and quarter-Jews [*Mischlinge*] who had been left so far relatively unaffected by the regime's anti-Jewish legislation.

Students also need to be aware of the *context* of the meeting, which had originally been scheduled for December 1941. By the time it was rescheduled for the following January, Germany's military and international situation was already causing concern. The attack on the Soviet Union had stalled in front of Moscow following the Soviet counter-attack in December. Germany had also declared war on the United States. There was no need to fear any immediate catastrophe, and the *Wehrmacht* would shortly prove that it was still capable of successfully retaking the offensive in Russia. However, Germany was now involved in a world war, and the longer it continued the less favourable its outlook would become. Hitler's 'prophecy' of January 1939, which had promised the annihilation of the Jewish race in Europe in the event of a world war, might well have been present in the minds of those who summoned the participants to Wannsee.

The biggest puzzle about the document is the *purpose* of the meeting it recorded. Some historians describe it as the meeting that 'authorised' the Holocaust, but this cannot be the case. For one thing, the participants – even Heydrich – were not sufficiently senior to make such a decision. In any case, as we saw in Chapter 6, if there ever was such a decision, Heydrich received his authority to call the meeting in a memorandum of 31 July 1941 written by Göring. It charged him with making 'all necessary preparations with regard to organisational, practical and financial aspects for an overall solution of the Jewish question in the German sphere of influence in Europe'. It is further proof of the relatively junior status of the Wannsee participants that none of the 'big beasts' of the regime – Hitler, Himmler, Goebbels or Göring himself – was present. In any case, the Holocaust had already begun. By January 1942, as we have seen, over a million Jews had already been murdered in the occupied Soviet Union. In December 1941, a month before the meeting at Wannsee, the first death camp had begun operation at Chelmno. The first death camp with fixed gassing installations, Belzec, was already under construction. It is overwhelmingly likely that the murder of Europe's Jews would have continued even if the conference had never taken place.

**National Socialist Racial Policy**

So what did those who called the meeting think it was about? According to Eichmann, the meeting had two main functions. The first was to assert tighter control over the genocide programme. Until Wannsee, he claimed, there had been 'too many obstacles and too many departments involved'. The meeting's second function was to assert Heydrich's personal authority over this key area of National Socialist policy. Heydrich certainly seems to have been satisfied with how the meeting went: Eichmann recorded that at its conclusion, Heydrich smoked a cigar and drank cognac, neither of which he normally did. Eichmann claimed that he too was well-satisfied with the conference: in his view, the 'popes had given their orders; it was up to me to obey, and that is what I bore in mind over the future years'. We need to be careful in evaluating Eichmann's statements: it was clearly in his interest, on trial for his life, to minimise his own role and to suggest that apart from strengthening Heydrich's position, the Wannsee meeting was not very important. Nonetheless, there is probably at least some truth in his view of the conference's purpose.

It is also worth asking what those who attended the meeting learned from doing so. It is clear that if they had not known or guessed it before, they knew by the end of the conference that a decision to kill all Europe's Jews had already been taken. They would have been left in no doubt that 'evacuation to the East' meant killing. They would have learned, too, that although the co-operation of the various ministries and agencies was seen as desirable, and even essential, the fact was that the SS was now in charge of the Final Solution. Heydrich in particular had now moved out of Himmler's shadow to assume a hitherto unknown independence in the execution of policy. The participants would also have discovered that the regime intended to solve the problem, left unresolved by the Nuremberg Laws of 1935, of Germans of mixed ancestry. But was it really necessary to hold a conference in order for these particular individuals to learn these things – many of which were perfectly well known at least to some of them?

**Looking At Documents:**

It may be that the best way to arrive at the meaning of this document is to study the list of participants. Almost every Party and state agency with any responsibility for Jewish questions was involved. This may suggest that Heydrich was interested, not so much in formulating policy, as in spreading the responsibility for carrying it out. The SS would command the genocide, but everyone else would also be involved. Even if the war went badly – which must have seemed a greater possibility than it had the previous summer – no one would later be able to claim that they had been ignorant. Those who attended the Wannsee conference became, whether they liked it or not, *Geheimnisträger* – the bearers of secrets. The Protocol is not a record of the meeting where the Holocaust was planned or authorised: that decision had already been made. But it captures the moment when most of the important agencies of the National Socialist regime accepted that eleven million people would be murdered over the next few years – and made no protest.

## 2. Himmler's Telephone Log

**30 November 1941**

**1.30 pm**

| Original | Translation |
|---|---|
| Verhaftung Dr Jekelius | Arrest of Dr Jekelius |
| Angebl. Sohn Molotow | Supposed son of Molotov |
| Judentransport aus Berlin | Jewish transport from Berlin |
| Keine Liquidierung | No liquidation |

**1 December 1941**

| | |
|---|---|
| Besuch bei Schwarz. | Visit from Schwarz. |
| Koksagys. | Koksagys. |
| Verwaltungsführer der SS haben zu bleiben. | Administrative leaders of the SS are to remain. |

*National Socialist Racial Policy*

Heinrich Himmler, *Reichsführer-SS* and Chief of the German Police, was a careful and thorough administrator. As a result, he was able to reach a position of almost unrivalled authority within the National Socialist regime. This thoroughness extended to his telephone calls. He noted the time of all the calls he made and received in a special log-book and, in his characteristic spiky handwriting, made a brief note of their subject-matter. His log-book survives, and the notes of two calls have aroused particular interest amongst historians. One was David Irving, who was found in a celebrated British libel case in 2000 to be a Holocaust denier and apologist for Hitler. In his 1977 book *Hitler's War,* he claimed that Himmler's telephone log proved that Hitler had forbidden the murder of the Jews. According to Irving,

> *Himmler was summoned to the Wolf's Lair for a secret conference with Hitler, at which the fate of Berlin's Jews was clearly raised. At 1:30 P.M. Himmler was obliged to telephone from Hitler's bunker to Heydrich the explicit order that Jews were* not *to be liquidated; and the next day Himmler telephoned SS General Oswald Pohl, overall chief of the concentration camp system, with the order: 'Jews are to stay where they are'.*

However, an unbiased reading of the telephone log does not support Irving's claims. There is no evidence in the log that Himmler was telephoning Heydrich – it is just as likely that Heydrich called Himmler – and it is mere supposition on Irving's part that the call was made after seeing Hitler. Indeed, more recent evidence suggests that Himmler met Hitler *after* the telephone call was made, thus making nonsense of Irving's assertion that Himmler was passing on a *Führer* order. An objective reading of the document would also suggest that the phrase 'No liquidation' referred only to the single transport of Jews from Berlin referred to in the line above. It is also possible, though less likely, that the reference to liquidation concerns Jekelius, who was on the transport and was believed by Himmler to be the son of Soviet foreign commissar Vyacheslav Molotov. It certainly cannot be interpreted as a ban on the liquidation of Jews in general, as Irving suggests. It is possible to find

**Looking At Documents:**

external corroboration for this. A single trainload of Jews was indeed sent from Berlin on 27 November to the Latvian capital of Riga, then under German occupation. No decision had yet been made about exactly what their fate should be. Himmler's telephone call may have reflected some lingering concern, at least at this stage, about murdering German Jews. Despite these reservations, on arrival in Riga on 30 November the Jews were offloaded by Friedrich Jeckeln, the local HSSPF, and immediately executed by machine-gunning. Himmler responded:

> The Jews who have been resettled out to the territory of the Ostland are only to be dealt with in accordance with guidelines issued by me or by the Reich Security Head Office on my authority. I will punish individual initiatives and contraventions.

But Jeckeln was not punished, and subsequent transports of Jews sent from Germany to Latvia went to the holding-camp at Salaspils, where almost all of them were eventually murdered.

If Irving was 'mistaken' about the entry for 30 November, what about his claim that the following day Himmler called Oswald Pohl with the order that the Jews were to sat where they were ? Here again, however, this claim does not bear scrutiny. It is clear that Himmler intended the administrative leaders of the SS to remain where they were: the entry does not mention Jews at all. Irving later admitted that he had simply 'misread' the word *haben* and read it as *Juden* [Jews]. This was not likely to have been an innocent mistake. It was in line with his claim that Hitler either knew nothing of the genocide or, when he did know, was anxious to prevent it. According to Irving, Hitler was the 'best friend the Jews had', a claim refuted by an overwhelming weight of evidence. In any case, there is a final and devastating flaw in the logic of Irving's argument. Let us assume that he was correct and that Hitler spoke to Himmler on 30 November 1941, ordering not just that one transport of Jews should not be liquidated, but that Jews in general should not be killed. This, according to Irving, was the instruction that Himmler passed on to Heydrich by telephone. But if Hitler ordered that Jews should not be liquidated, it would be a reasonable assumption that he knew that this was at least a strong possibility. In fact, as we saw in Chapter 6, he had been kept well-informed of the progress of the mass murder in Russia that had accompanied *Barbarossa*. And if Hitler ordered merely that a particular transport of Berlin Jews should not be liquidated, this suggests equally strongly that he was making an exception in this particular case, and knew that the majority of Jews transported to the East faced execution on arrival. So the telephone log of Heinrich Himmler cannot be used to deny the reality of the Holocaust. Nor does it in any way remove from Hitler knowledge of, and responsibility for, the crimes of the National Socialist regime.

**Looking At Documents:**

# Glossary

**Ahnenerbe**: Ancestral Heritage: An SS agency concerned with researching the origins and history of the Nordic peoples.

**Aktion Reinhardt/Reinhard:** The operation of the three death-camps on or near the river Bug in Poland during 1942/43 – Sobibor, Belzec and Treblinka – was known as *Aktion Reinhardt*, later renamed *Reinhard* in honour of Reinhard Heydrich, RSHA chief and acting Protector of Bohemia-Moravia, who was assassinated in May 1942.

**Aryan**: A prehistoric tribal group from northern India or central Asia. In Germanic fantasy: an early race of Nordic super-beings who were the original creators of civilisation.

**Auschwitz-Birkenau**: A complex of camps in the Krakow area of Poland. Some of the camps held slave labourers, but the largest, Auschwitz II or Birkenau, was used as a mass-killing centre, overwhelmingly for Jews. An estimated 1.1 million people died in the Auschwitz complex between 1942 and 1945.

**Brown House**: The headquarters of the NSDAP in Munich.

***Barbarossa***: Codename for the German attack on the Soviet Union of 22 June 1941.

**Commissar Order**: A directive signed in June 1941 by Reinhard Heydrich, authorising the execution of Soviet state and party officials captured during the forthcoming invasion of the USSR.

**Concentration camp**: *Konzentrationlager,* or *KZ*. Camps for political and other enemies of the regime. The first was set up at Dachau, near Munich, in 1933. They were quite separate from the death camps set up for the murder of Jews and other racial groups. This confusion arose at the end of the war, when many concentration camps did contain death camp prisoners evacuated there from the East.

**Death marches**: At the beginning of 1945, those camps in the East which still functioned were emptied of their prisoners, who were moved west. This seems to have been to avoid such large numbers of witnesses falling into Soviet hands. Owing to the brutality with which the marches were conducted, the freezing conditions and the poor physical condition of the prisoners, huge numbers of them died.

**Dreyfus Affair**: A French political and social scandal, lasting from 1895 until 1907. Alfred Dreyfus, a French officer of Jewish origin, was falsely accused of having sold military secrets to Germany and imprisoned on Devil's Island. Although it became clear that another officer was guilty, the evidence was suppressed for many years until Dreyfus's eventual release and pardon. The Affair provided graphic evidence of the strength of anti-Semitism in France.

**Einsatzgruppen**: Task Groups. Mobile task forces of SS and police personnel under the authority of Reichsführer-SS Heinrich Himmler, which in Poland and the USSR carried out the mass-murder of those seen as hostile to the occupying forces, particularly Jews.

**Erbkranke**: Hereditarily ill. Those classified under this heading included many people suffering from mental or physical handicaps. Also included were other social categories such as alcoholics, the 'asocial' and the 'work-shy'.

**Eugenics**: A now largely discredited social philosophy advocating the improvement of hereditary traits in a group or society through selective breeding. Eugenics was especially popular in the first half of the twentieth century and partly put into practice in several countries, including Germany, Sweden and the United States.

**Euthanasia Programme**: Known as *Aktion T-4*. The murder of first German, and then Polish individuals believed to be suffering from hereditary mental and physical illnesses, which began in August 1939 and continued, despite officially being abandoned in 1942, until the end of the war. It was headed by Philipp Bouhler, who was also head of the Führer Chancellery [*Kanzlei des Führers*].

**Final Solution**: *Endlösung*. One of a number of similar euphemisms used by the National Socialist regime as cover for the mass-murder of Europe's Jews.

**Functionalism**: A historiographical approach to the study of National Socialist racial policy which believes that policy was improvised and reflected the input of a wide variety and level of decision-maker. Examples of functionalist historians are Martin Broszat, Ulrich Herbert and Ian Kershaw.

**Gau**: [plural: *Gaue*] Party region. The NSDAP divided Germany for administrative and political puposes into *Gaue*, each of which was led by a *Gauleiter*. A few *Gaue* were large enough to make those who ran them important figures in their own right: Berlin's *Gauleiter* was Propaganda minister Josef Goebbels.

**Generalplan-Ost**: A plan for the re-ordering of Europe along racial and ethnic lines. The Plan was produced by the RSHA. A final version was completed in 1940 and approved by Adolf Hitler the following year. The plan involved large-scale population transfers, ethnic cleansing and mass murder.

**Genocide**: A crime, or any one of a number of crimes, defined by the 1948 United Nations Convention on Genocide as 'committed with the intention to destroy, in whole or in part, a national, ethical, racial or religious group as such'. These crimes include, but are not limited to, killing; causing serious bodily or mental harm to the group; imposing conditions of life so extreme that they are likely to bring about the destruction of the group; preventing births or forcibly transferring children from one group to another.

**General-Government**: A German-run area of central and southern Poland created in 1939 from territories neither directly incorporated into Germany nor annexed by the USSR.

**Ghetto**: An enclosed area of compulsory residence for Jews, common in medieval Europe and re-established in the major cities of Eastern Europe under German jurisdiction.

**Gleichschaltung**: co-ordination. The process of adjusting to National Socialist rule after 30 January 1933.

**GPU**: [*Gosudarstvennoye Politicheskoye Upravleniye*]. Acronym for State Political Directorate, the Soviet secret police from 1922–1934.

**Gulag**: [*Glavnoye Upravleniye Ispravityelno-Trudovikh **Lagerey***]. Soviet acronym for the Chief Administration of Corrective Labour Camps and Colonies.

**Historikerstreit**: Historians' conflict: A historical debate from the 1980s, triggered by Ernst Nolte's claim that the Holocaust was a 'response' to events in the Soviet Union.

**HSSPF**: *Höhere SS- und Polizei Führer*, Higher SS and Police Leader.

**Holocaust**: From the Greek term, 'wholly consumed by fire', this has come to be the standard term for the mass-murder of Europe's Jews, though the term is sometimes also extended to cover other mass-murders and crimes committed by the National Socialist regime.

**Holocaust denial**: Claiming or asserting that there was no systematic attempt by the National Socialist regime to murder Europe's Jews; that the number of victims has been exaggerated; that no death camps existed, and that there is no evidence for the existence of homicidal gas chambers. Usually politically inspired, Holocaust denial must ignore, distort or raise implausible doubts about the overwhelming mass of evidence to the contrary, most of it provided by the regime itself.

**Intentionalism**: A historiographical approach to the study of National Socialist racial policy. It holds that policy was consistent and directed from above, and in particular by Adolf Hitler.

*National Socialist Racial Policy*

Intentionalists believe that racial policy was from the beginning genocidal in intention. Intentionalist historians include Lucy S. Dawidowicz and Gerald Fleming.

**Jewish Council**: *Judenrat*. Jewish communities under German control were often led by councils composed of Jews picked out for the purpose. To a limited and strictly controlled extent, Jewish communities were 'run by their own', but this should not conceal the obvious fact that real power lay with the German administration.

**Lebensborn**: Well of Life. An SS agency which organised pre- and ante-natal care facilities for the mothers of racially acceptable offspring born out of wedlock.

**Lebensraum**: Living-space.

**Łódz**: A large industrial city in central Poland. Renamed Litzmannstadt under German occupation, its Jewish population was second in size only to that of Warsaw. Its Jewish ghetto was run with dictatorial efficiency in 1940-44 by Mordecai Chaim Rumkowski.

**Madagascar Plan**: A short-lived proposal to empty Europe of Jews by relocating them to the Indian Ocean island of Madagascar.

**Mischling:** [plural: *Mischlinge*]: A person of mixed Jewish and 'Aryan' ancestry.

**NSDAP**: *Nationalsozialistische Deutsche Arbeiter Partei*: National Socialist German Workers' Party: the ruling political organisation in Germany 1933-45.

**Nazi**: The customary abbreviation for National Socialist. This book avoids it on the grounds that the use of this nickname can help to trivialise National Socialism and prevent us from fully grasping its importance.

**Nisko Plan**: A Jewish reservation established at Nisko, near Lublin in occupied Poland, between September 1939 and March 1940.

**Nuremberg Laws**: Laws passed in September 1935 which included the Law for the Preservation of German Blood and German Honour and the Reich Citizenship Law. These laws for the first time, officially defined what it meant to be Jewish. They also forbade sexual relations between 'Aryans' and Jews.

**OKH**: *Oberkommando des Heeres*: High Command of the Army.

**Ostjuden**: Eastern Jews. Jews of Polish or Russian origin.

**Ostland**: A *Reichskommissariat* or Eastern territory, consisting of the former Baltic states and parts of modern Belarus, seized from the Soviet Union in 1941.

**Partisans:** Members of the armed forces of a particular state who continue to fight even after their district or region has been occupied. The term partisan is almost always used to describe resistance groups in Eastern and Southern Europe during the Second World War.

**Plutocracy**: Rule by the wealthy.

**Pogrom**: A violent and sustained assault on a Jewish community, sometimes – though not always – condoned by the authorities.

**Protocols of the Elders of Zion**: A forged document which emerged in Russia at the beginning of the twentieth century, and was widely disseminated throughout Europe after the First World War. It was almost certainly produced on the orders of Pyotr I. Rachkovsky, head of the *Okhrana* – the tsarist secret police. The document claimed to be the master-plan of the Jews for world domination.

**Prussia**: *Preußen*. By far the largest German state, established as an independent kingdom in 1700 and the central element of the united Germany created in 1871. In 1945 most of Prussia was ceded to Poland or the USSR, while the western areas were distributed amongst the re-created states of the Federal Republic in 1949. Prussia officially ceased to exist in 1947.

**RuSHA**: *Rasse - & Siedlungshauptamt*, Race and Settlement Main Office. An SS agency responsible, initially, for ensuring the racial purity of members of the SS, but which gradually acquired numerous other responsibilities.

**Reichskristallnacht**: The Night of Broken Glass. This took place on 9/10 November 1938 and was a nationwide anti-Jewish pogrom directed by Josef Goebbels in the wake of the assassination of a German diplomat in Paris by a Jewish émigré. Thousands of

Jews were arrested, many were killed and much Jewish property was destroyed.

**RSHA**: *Reichssicherheitshauptamt*. Reich Security Main Office. The principal security directorate of National Socialist Germany. It was subordinated to the SS but contained the *Gestapo* [*Geheime Staatspolizei*: Secret State Police] *Kripo* [*Kriminalpolizei*: Criminal Police] *Sipo* [*Sicherheitspolizei*: Security Police] and the SD [*Sicherheitsdienst*: Security Service], which was the SS security service. Set up in 1939, it was run by Reinhard Heydrich and, after his assassination in 1942, by Ernst Kaltenbrunner.

**'Rhineland Bastards'**: A derogatory term for the offspring of German mothers and French African soldiers from the army occupying the Rhineland after 1919. Widely perceived as symbolic of French attempts to shame Germans by encouraging racial mixing, there were calls for action against them as early as the 1920s. Over 400 were sterilised after 1939.

**Romani**: More accurately known as the Roma and Sinti, and also known, derogatorily, as 'Gipsies' or 'Gypsies'. Of Indian origin, the Romani entered Europe in the twelfth century and were soon widely distributed there. Their nomadic lifestyle and 'inferior' race led to persecution in many parts of Europe and has continued to this day. National Socialist policy towards them was not always consistent. A decision to kill most, if not all, the Romani under German rule was made by Himmler in 1942.

**Schizophrenia**: A severe mental disorder, resulting in fractured perceptions of reality. A tendency to schizophrenia may be partly hereditary, although environmental factors are also significant.

**Sorb**: A group of ethnic Slavs, resident since the seventh century in the Lausitz area of Germany [modern Brandenburg and Saxony]. During the National Socialist period there were attempts to Germanise them, and activists for a distinctively Sorb identity were persecuted.

**SPD**: *Sozialdemokratische Partei Deutschlands*. Social Democratic Party of Germany.

**SS**: *Schutzstaffel*. Protection Units. Initially simply Adolf Hitler's personal bodyguard, it became an elite order, with its own security, policy and military units [*Waffen-SS*]. It was led by *Reichsführer-SS* Heinrich Himmler. Its *Totenkopfverbände* [Death's Head Groups] ran the concentration camps. Almost all sub-groups within the SS were involved in the mass-murder of Europe's Jews. Declared a criminal organisation by the Allies in 1945.

**SD**: *Sicherheitsdienst*. The Security Service of the SS. Set up to combat enemies both within and beyond the NSDAP.

**Sipo**: *Sicherheitspolizei*. Security Police

**Third Reich**: National Socialist Germany was often, though un-officially, described as the Third Reich – *Reich* meaning 'empire'. The first Reich was established in the Middle Ages, especially un-der the Saxon and Hohenstaufen emperors. The Second Reich was established in 1871, and lasted until its collapse in 1918.

**Volk**: Can be translated as 'people'; but this conceals the racial and ethnic dimension implicit in the German term.

**Volksgemeinschaft**: Racial community.

**Wannsee Conference**: Held on 20 January 1942 at Wannsee on the outskirts of Berlin, this was an inter-departmental conference that met to co-ordinate the 'final solution to the Jewish problem'. Chaired by Reinhard Heydrich, it effectively asserted SS control over the ongoing genocide.

**Warthegau**: An area of central Poland, containing the city of Łódz, directly annexed to the German Reich in 1939.

**Wehrmacht**: The regular German army.

---

# Further Reading

THERE ARE MANY BOOKS on the National Socialist regime and, in contrast with the situation described in Chapter 1, nowadays most deal with at least some aspect of racial policy. Rather than provide a lengthy and intimidating list, the author has selected a small number which would be particularly useful for students. They provide either a helpful overview or they explore key areas in detail.

**The Racial State: Germany 1933 – 1945** *Michael Burleigh and Wolfgang Wippermann, Cambridge University Press 1991.*

This is an indispensable overview of the topic, managing to cover almost every aspect of racial policy, from its origins to its implementation. The book helps to answer one of the key questions raised by historians about National Socialism: was it a reactionary phenomenon, or can it more truly be described as revolutionary?

*The main object of social policy remained the creation of a hierarchical racial new order. Everything else was subordinate to this goal, including the regime's conduct of foreign affairs and the war. In the eyes of the regime's racial politicians, the Second World War was above all a racial war, to be pursued with immense brutality until the end; that is until the concentration camps were liberated by invading Allied armies. All of these points draw attention to the specific and singular character of the Third Reich. It was not a form of regression to past times. Its objects were novel and sui generis★: to realise an ideal future world, without 'lesser races', without the sick, and without those whom they decreed had no place in the 'national community'. It was a regime without precedent or parallel.*
★*sui generis* [Latin] of its own kind – unique, special.

**The Holocaust In History** *Michael R Marrus, Penguin 1987*

Despite being over twenty years old, this survey of the Jewish dimension of racial policy remains an excellent starting-point for students: it is clear, accessible and well–organised, with important sections on often neglected areas such as European public opinion. As the title indicates, the book also looks at the Holocaust as a historiographical phenomenon, and traces how historians have studied it in the years since the events themselves. Marrus is particularly interested in the question of whether the Holocaust can be studied as if it were a 'normal' historical event. This question is every bit as contentious now as when he was writing in 1987:

*Not everyone is happy, of course. To some, the academic tone adopted by some who have written on the Holocaust is itself a violation. They fear that the use of professional historical discourse will turn the Holocaust into a subject like any other, robbing it of its historical uniqueness. Others fear vulgarisation – a tendency to exploit the Holocaust for political or aesthetic reasons or to make a trivial point. Clearly, however, it is the historians' task to guard against distortions as well as to discover truth. Can those who write history be trusted with the Holocaust?*

*My own view is that we have little choice but to do so. For better or worse, we shall have to rely increasingly upon historians to transmit what is known about the massacre of European Jewry. No one else is likely to do so in a way which commands credibility and standing in our culture. But as historians convey their accounts, no one should expect them to do so with one voice, or with a single perspective.*

**The Diary of Dawid Sierakowiak: Five Notebooks from the Łódz Ghetto** *Edited by Alan Adelson, Bloomsbury 1996*

This is a remarkable historical document: as the title indicates, it comes from the Łódz Ghetto, and was written by an eighteen-year old student who remorselessly recorded the increasing pressure on every aspect of life in the ghetto. He himself did not survive, and his diary, discovered by chance after the war, contains virtually all that is known about him. Its value as a source lies in its clear demonstration of the tensions and disagreements within the Jewish community. Here, Jews are not one-dimensional 'victims'; they are ordinary people caught up in extraordinary circumstances, who cannot know that most will not survive. In some ways it is a more revealing source than Anne Frank's diary, because Sierakowiak's experience was far more typical of the Jewish experience, especially in Eastern Europe.

**National Socialist Racial Policy**

*Monday May 25 1942*
*There are no vegetables in the June ration, not even potatoes. Now Rum-*
*kowski won't have to bother himself that people have eaten their potatoes*
*too early: we won't even have a chance to see them this time. The situa-*
*tion is worsening, and there is no hope for the end.*
*They keep relocating Jews from small neighbouring towns into the ghetto,*
*while the deportations have stopped. Even that chance for getting out of*
*the ghetto has been taken away. Death is striking right and left. A per-*
*son becomes thin – an 'hourglass' – and pale in the face, then comes the*
*swelling, a few days in bed or in the hospital, and that's it. The person*
*was living, the person is dead: we live and die like cattle.*

## Into That Darkness: From Mercy-Killing to Mass Murder
*Gitta Sereny Pimlico 1995*
This is an extraordinary book. The author, Gitta Sereny, has also
written about Albert Speer, Hitler's architect and armaments minister. In the early 1970s Sereny spent many hours interviewing Franz
Stangl. Stangl was then serving a life sentence in a German prison,
having been convicted of mass murder. Stangl's first involvement
in racial policy was as part the *Aktion T-4* euthanasia programme;
from there he went to Poland, where he was successively in charge
of the Sobibor and Treblinka death camps. Through her questioning, Sereny was able to establish just how Stangl had made the key
decisions that affected first his life, and then those of hundreds of
thousands of others.
So you didn't feel they were human beings?
*'Cargo,' he said tonelessly, 'They were cargo'. He raised and dropped his*
*hand in a gesture of despair. Both our voices had dropped.*
When do you think you began to think of them as cargo? The
way you spoke earlier, of the day when you first came to Treblinka, the horror you felt seeing the dead bodies everywhere – they
weren't cargo to you then, were they?
*'I think it started the day I saw the* Totenlager *[the area containing the*
*gas chambers] in Treblinka. I remember Wirth standing there, next to the*
*pits full of blue-black corpses. It had nothing to do with humanity – it*

**Further Reading**

couldn't have; it was a mass – a mass of rotting flesh. Wirth said, "What shall we do with this garbage?" I think unconsciously that started me thinking of them as cargo.'

There were so many children, did they ever make you think of your children, of how you would feel in the position of those parents?

'No', he said slowly, 'I can't say I ever thought that way'. He paused. 'You see,' he then continued, still speaking with this extreme seriousness and obviously intent on finding a new truth within himself, 'I rarely saw them as individuals. It was always a huge mass. I sometimes stood on the wall and saw them in the tube [the path leading to the gas chambers]. But – how can I explain it – they were naked, packed together, running, being driven with whips like…'. Stangl's voice trailed off.

www.ingramcontent.com/pod-product-compliance
Lightning Source LLC
LaVergne TN
LVHW051555080426
835510LV00020B/2995